Educational Research and Innovation

Promoting Education Decision Makers' Use of Evidence in Flanders

Claire Shewbridge and Florian Köster

This work is published under the responsibility of the Secretary-General of the OECD. The opinions expressed and arguments employed herein do not necessarily reflect the official views of the Members of the OECD.

This document, as well as any data and map included herein, are without prejudice to the status of or sovereignty over any territory, to the delimitation of international frontiers and boundaries and to the name of any territory, city or area.

Please cite this publication as:
Shewbridge, C. and F. Köster (2021), *Promoting Education Decision Makers' Use of Evidence in Flanders*, Educational Research and Innovation, OECD Publishing, Paris, *https://doi.org/10.1787/de604fde-en*.

ISBN 978-92-64-68198-9 (print)
ISBN 978-92-64-89611-6 (pdf)

Educational Research and Innovation
ISSN 2076-9660 (print)
ISSN 2076-9679 (online)

Photo credits: Cover © Milan M/Shutterstock.com.

Corrigenda to publications may be found on line at: *www.oecd.org/about/publishing/corrigenda.htm*.
© OECD 2021

The use of this work, whether digital or print, is governed by the Terms and Conditions to be found at *http://www.oecd.org/termsandconditions*.

Foreword

There are many minds and hearts involved in designing and delivering Flemish education – and yet more who have passionate opinions on how children and young people should benefit from this. This OECD case study finds that a shared concern binds them together: how can we improve the quality of education? It is a pivotal moment in Flemish education, with plans to introduce standardised tests in primary and secondary schools over the coming years. The OECD Strategic education governance team was invited to consult with stakeholders and provide analysis against its research-based framework on whether and how the introduction of standardised tests could best support this collective aim to improve the quality of education.

OECD work on strategic education governance supports countries in identifying the best ways to achieve national objectives for education systems in a context of multi-level governance structures and complex environments. Informed by empirical research, the strategic education governance framework can help policy makers bring effective governance processes onto the political agenda. It identifies and promotes six interrelated domains that collectively promote more effective governance processes: accountability, capacity, knowledge governance, stakeholder involvement, strategic thinking and a whole-of-system perspective. In each domain, research underpins a set of core principles.

For strategic education governance case studies, the OECD develops questions linked to the core principles in each domain of the framework and/or gives emphasis to one particular domain. Case study questions are adapted to individual contexts and priorities, but anchored in the common research-based framework providing countries with a set of aspirational efforts for self-reflection. The OECD case study offers a common language to enable sharing of local practices and to promote dialogue among stakeholders.

Stakeholder involvement is a pillar of the strategic education governance framework. This OECD case study on the introduction of standardised tests in Flanders places the perceptions, hopes and concerns of key stakeholders at the centre of the analysis. It collects feedback from key stakeholders via a series of structured discussions and a stakeholder reflection seminar. Anchored in the strategic education governance framework, the OECD case study aims to gauge areas for further investigation and inform thinking about possible next practices. It is designed as a conversation starter on how to optimise the processes around the development of standardised tests.

Acknowledgements

This report presents input from key stakeholders regarding the introduction of standardised tests in Flanders. The OECD team extends heartfelt gratitude to all those who gave time to provide valuable insights to their perceptions, hopes and concerns during structured interviews (February and March 2021) and the stakeholder reflection seminar (June 2021). The OECD team enjoyed constructive and open discussions with all participants and is grateful for the frank and trusting exchanges. Our learning was in no way impaired by the virtual nature of the discussions, but we sincerely hope to continue learning together in person in the future. We are equally grateful to those who took time to provide written responses and send supporting evidence.

This report was prepared as part of the strategic education governance project within the OECD Centre for Educational Research and Innovation (CERI). The OECD team is indebted to the Flemish Department for Education and Training (DOV) for the opportunity to engage in the case study and support CERI's work applying lessons from research to promote strategic education governance. We are grateful to Jeroen Backs and Miekatrien Sterck for the initial guidance and provision of contacts for key stakeholders and to Bieke De Fraine for taking up the co-ordination responsibilities and providing timely and pertinent feedback on the draft report.

The structured discussions with key stakeholders were conducted by Claire Shewbridge and Florian Köster. Claire Shewbridge led the analysis and drafting of the report. The report is anchored in the strategic education governance framework, which was collectively developed by a core team of Claire Shewbridge, Florian Köster and Rien Rouw. The strategic education governance framework allows the application of a body of CERI work on governance in complex education systems, led by Tracey Burns, with her team Marc Fuster and Florian Köster. For the strategic education governance framework, Florian Köster developed the conceptual framework for the systematic use of evidence by decision makers (Chapter 5), based on work by Laurenz Langer, Janice Tripney and David Gough. Florian Köster, with support from Glenn Fahey, prepared the conceptual underpinnings for the framework on accountability (Chapter 6). Clara Krämer initiated work on how to operationalise strategic thinking (Chapter 4). All areas of the strategic education governance framework have been enriched by the knowledge, expertise and policy experience of Rien Rouw, with a special thank you for his input to operationalising our framework on stakeholder involvement (Chapter 3).

Many thanks to Leonora Lynch-Stein for her management of the layout and publication process, to Sophie Limoges for editiorial support and to Giannina Rech for compiling the Programme for International Student Assessment (PISA) trends data in Chapter 4.

Table of contents

Foreword — 3

Acknowledgements — 4

Executive Summary — 7

1 Introduction to the case study — 9
    Introduction — 10
    References — 11

2 Strategic education governance and case study methods — 13
    Strategic education governance — 14
    Case study methods — 15
    References — 18

3 Stakeholder involvement — 19
    Stakeholder involvement as a cornerstone of strategic education governance — 20
    Stakeholder involvement at the initial stages to develop standardised tests — 22
    Stakeholder perceptions of their involvement at the initial stages — 23
    Developments in stakeholder involvement — 25
    References — 26

4 Strategic thinking and whole-of-system perspective — 27
    Strategic thinking and whole-of-system perspective — 28
    A shared concern on the overall quality of education in Flanders — 29
    A complex debate on educational quality and concerns for equity — 33
    Support for standardised tests as tools for school development — 36
    References — 38

5 Capacity and knowledge governance — 40
    Capacity — 41
    Capacity for test development, administration and school quality assurance — 41
    Knowledge governance: promoting the systematic use of evidence — 46
    Motivations and capabilities for using the results of standardised tests — 47
    References — 53

6 Accountability — 54
    Accountability — 55

Accountability in Flanders and the introduction of standardised tests	56
References	62

7 Lessons from the OECD case study 65

Stakeholder involvement (Chapter 3)	66
Strategic thinking and whole-of-system perspective (Chapter 4)	67
Capacity and knowledge governance (Chapter 5)	68
Accountability (Chapter 6)	69

FIGURES

Figure 2.1. Domains of strategic education governance	14
Figure 3.1. OECD mapping of stakeholders and key elements related to standardised tests	21
Figure 3.2. Timeline of initial stakeholder involvement	22
Figure 4.1. Primary education: evidence from national sample assessments	30
Figure 4.2. Secondary education: evidence from national sample assessments at Grade 8	32
Figure 4.3. Secondary education: evidence from the OECD's PISA (students aged 15)	33
Figure 4.4. Secondary education: feedback from school leaders on school admission policies	35
Figure 4.5. Openness to change: feedback from teachers and school leaders	37
Figure 5.1. School leaders' perceptions of school capacity related to digital devices (DD)	44
Figure 5.2. Quality assurance capacity in Flemish primary and secondary schools	45
Figure 5.3. Promoting the systematic use of evidence by decision makers	47
Figure 6.1. Generating learning through constructive accountability relationships	55
Figure 6.2. The triangle of educational quality in Flanders	59

TABLES

Table 2.1. OECD case study individual structured discussions with stakeholders	15
Table 4.1. Primary education: changes in average performance in international assessments	31
Table 4.2. Primary education: changes in performance distribution in international assessments	31
Table 4.3. Primary education: performance in different content areas of international assessments	31
Table 4.4. Feedback from educators on the prestige of the teaching profession and stress levels	34
Table 4.5. Secondary education: feedback from school leaders on staff qualification and shortages	35
Table 5.1. Toolkit of validated tests for use by primary schools	42
Table 5.2. Expectations for school quality assurance capacity in Flemish schools	44
Table 5.3. Flemish student perceptions of teacher feedback (PISA 2018)	48
Table 5.4. Stakeholder perceptions on opportunities the standardised tests could offer	49
Table 5.5. Feedback from the stakeholder seminar on necessary preparations	52

Executive Summary

Despite evolving attitudes over the past ten years in Flemish education, there is room to improve the availability and use of data at the school level. The current government plans to introduce central standardised tests in 2024. Based on a feasibility study, considerations of different scenarios for standardised tests are ongoing, including purposes, reporting and administration. The Flemish department of education and training invited the OECD to consult with stakeholders on their motivations and concerns. Presenting stakeholder feedback and supporting evidence in six interrelated domains of a research-based strategic education governance framework, the analysis identifies several lessons for the further work.

Stakeholder involvement

Prioritising clear and active communication: The high-level forum can serve as an authoritative communication channel and also collect feedback in a timely and transparent way from key stakeholders. There is opportunity to more actively involve stakeholders in the next stage of development, such as to provide input into clarifying the purpose(s) and uses of the standardised tests. This will enable stakeholders to take up their roles and responsibilities in preparing for the introduction of standardised tests.

Committing to stakeholder involvement and ensuring key voices are heard: An important lesson is to take stakeholder involvement seriously at every stage of the policy development. Mobilising awareness, support and feedback channels for school leaders will be critical. Supporting a student survey on their expectations of standardised tests will empower student voice and provide pertinent insights.

Organising contributions from the educational field to support the university centre: There is motivation for involvement in test development and opportunity in establishing a coalition of test development partners across educational networks. The university centre can facilitate this by providing clear guidance on scheduling and expected time commitments.

Strategic thinking and whole-of-system perspective

Developing, sharing and consolidating common goals and how standardised tests will support these: The OECD case study has found a shared concern on the overall quality of education in Flanders and a body of evidence to support this. Such widespread recognition is pivotal and presents an opportunity to create a common vision for the role of standardised tests. There is strong support for standardised tests as tools to support school quality development and it is important to consider safeguard measures to this effect, including to ensure schools are encouraged to continue to develop and innovate their practice.

Taking a long-term perspective and adapting to changing contexts and new knowledge: There is value in refining and evolving the standardised tests development through concrete experiences in the educational field. This brings opportunities for professional learning and development through the collaboration of the research community (test developers) and schools. The first administrations of the standardised tests will generate much knowledge on how to optimise the use of results at the school level.

An opportunity to clarify initial expectations is to ensure a coherent approach and communication from the Flemish education inspectorate and the pedagogical advisory services on how to use these results for school development as part of the broader view of educational quality (the 'OK' quality framework).

Coordinating action and learning from experiences in the educational field: There is value in providing coordinated guidance from the central authorities, based on systematic input from the educational field, on the expected use of the standardised tests and the associated time and resource requirements for teachers and schools.

Capacity and knowledge governance

Ensuring technical capacity for standardised test development and administration: Strong credibility for the university centre as a centre of scientific expertise will provide fertile ground for gaining regular feedback from the educational field during test development. There will need to be a careful evaluation of schools' capacity to administer digital tests and due attention to field trials.

Laying foundations for the systematic use of standardised test results by professionals, with attention to:

Skills - There is a need to give adequate attention to the capabilities of teachers and other school staff to work with the results of standardised tests and other assessments. There is opportunity in committing to investment in professional development and in ways that can support collaborative practices in schools.

Availability - The rapidity of results feedback will play into their perceived value and relevance for educators. Notably, this would support students' expectations for the standardised tests to bolster the culture of feedback to students on their progress more generally.

Organisational processes - School leaders will drive the preparation of the necessary processes and structures to create the space for effective use of the standardised tests. This can be supported at the system level by preparation of common guidance material for schools – a process that will need to engage school leaders and teachers and mobilise the expertise of pedagogical advisory services.

Interaction - The design and development of feedback from the standardised tests will be strengthened by the direct interaction between researchers and schools. Importantly, this presents an opportunity to promote horizontal collaboration and learning across the different educational networks.

Standards - The development of guidance material for schools will provide a common anchor for expectations on the use of standardised tests, clarifying how they are connected with the existing central anchors of the attainment targets and the broader 'OK' quality framework. There are roles here for the Flemish education inspectorate and the pedagogical advisory services to document expectations of how schools can interpret and position the data from the standardised tests in a broader array of evidence.

Accountability

Ensuring the 'fit' of accountability instruments: The OECD case study has noted the perception of 'accountability' in Flemish education as a matter of internal responsibility and great resistance to the public availability of school performance information. There is opportunity to place standardised tests within the strengths of the current accountability system that focuses on dialogue and deepening an understanding between available data and links to ideas for improving practice.

Enhancing critical reflection on substantive expectations: Data from standardised tests will provide an objective and external perspective for school development, with appropriate mechanisms for designing data use and interpretation by teachers and school leaders to support informed practice and strategic planning. The inspectorate can confer a valuable perspective to schools on how they use the results.

1 Introduction to the case study

This chapter provides a brief introduction to the OECD case study on the introduction of standardised tests in Flanders.

Introduction

In Belgium, the constitution guarantees 'freedom of education'. Flemish schools enjoy the highest levels of autonomy among OECD countries in all aspects of education, including assessment practices. Flemish schools affiliate with umbrella organisations, many of which offer curricula and assessment supports via pedagogical advisory services. Schools can choose whether to use these services, including student assessments. There are no central examinations for students at the end of compulsory education in Flanders – an approach shared by only a handful of OECD countries (OECD, 2016[1]).

Flanders does administer some sample-based student assessments. In OECD countries, the use of standardised assessments in primary and secondary education is commonplace and over the past twenty years, the majority of OECD countries have chosen to administer census-based assessments, that is, with all students and schools participating (OECD, 2015[2]). Flanders introduced central assessments in 2002 and chose to assess only a sample of schools in each assessment. The sample-based central assessment (the 'peilingen') tests 1500 to 3000 students in different learning areas based on the expected level of learning, as specified in the central attainment targets. Each assessment round tests different learning areas on a rotating basis. All Flemish schools can choose to administer a parallel version of the central assessments (paralleltoets), but the uptake is low.

Just over ten years ago, OECD data from PISA indicated that standardised tests were not very present in Flemish secondary schools. In PISA 2009, three-quarters of the participating Flemish students were in schools that never used standardised tests, according to reports by their school leaders – and virtually none in schools providing parents with information on how their child's performance compared to central benchmarks (OECD, 2010[3]). In 2010, an OECD review on school evaluation in Flanders found broad agreement in the educational field that central standardised tests would not be valuable for Flemish schools (Shewbridge et al., 2011[4]).

However, over the past ten years, there is some evidence that the reality in the educational field has evolved. In PISA 2015, over half of the participating Flemish students were in schools that reported using some form of standardised tests, and in the majority of cases these were used to compare school performance to other schools or to a performance benchmark at a local or central level (OECD, 2016[1]). Research in 2016/17 found an opening of minds to the potential benefits of standardised tests in Flemish schools (Penninckx et al., 2017[5]). The idea of using student assessments (all types) to monitor school progress from year to year has also taken root: two-thirds of participating Flemish students in PISA 2018 were in schools where this was reportedly the case (OECD, 2020[6]).

Since 2018/19, primary schools are required to administer tests to students in Grade 6 and must choose from a toolkit of validated tests, which includes the central parallel tests and tests developed by two of the umbrella organisations for schools. Already in 2015/16, the vast majority of affiliated schools chose to administer tests developed by these umbrella organisations (Janssen et al., 2017[7]).

Despite these evolutions, the Flemish education inspectorate still finds the need to improve the reliability and objectivity of school quality assurance processes in both primary and secondary education (Chapter 5). There is room to improve the availability and use of data at the school level. The current government plans to introduce central standardised tests in 2024. The proposal to introduce standardised tests was included in part of the political manifesto. The government launched a feasibility study in September 2020. The feasibility study looked to map out different scenarios for the design and use of standardised tests, including the key design features of purpose, reporting and administration.

Considerations of the different scenarios for standardised tests are ongoing. The Minister established a high-level forum in May to facilitate communication and feedback among stakeholders on policy decisions at key stages of the development of standardised tests. At the end of September 2021, the high-level forum received a preparatory text with proposals, based on the feasibility study. The first administration of standardised tests will be in May 2024, in Grades 4 and 8. In May 2023, there will be a field trial to evaluate the difficulty level of each item in the tests. The schedule is to introduce standardised tests in Grade 6 for May 2026 and in Grade 12 for May 2027.

The Flemish Department of Education and Training invited the OECD strategic education governance team to consult with stakeholders on their perceptions, hopes and concerns about the introduction of standardised tests. This reflects the department's priority in 2021 to engage in communication efforts and dialogue with stakeholders. The OECD case study involved two main data collection channels: a series of structured discussions with key stakeholders in February and March, and a stakeholder reflection seminar in June.

This report presents feedback gathered from stakeholders as part of the OECD case study. It uses a research-based framework for strategic education governance (Chapter 2), that was the anchor for structured discussions with stakeholders and presents results as follows:

- Stakeholder involvement (Chapter 3): The OECD case study documents feedback from stakeholders on how they perceived their involvement in the early stages of the project to develop standardised tests and how they can contribute going forward.
- Strategic thinking and whole-of-system perspective (Chapter 4): Taking a step back from their daily responsibilities, stakeholders identify and comment on concerns and opportunities for the Flemish education system overall and the role that standardised tests might play in addressing these.
- Capacity and knowledge governance (Chapter 5): Stakeholders provide feedback on more concrete aspects regarding the introduction of standardised tests. This includes considerations about existing capacity for testing and quality assurance in the educational field. Stakeholders also identify the opportunities that the introduction of standardised tests may bring for their work and the necessary preparations to ensure the standardised tests support educational quality.
- Accountability (Chapter 6): Stakeholders provide feedback on the current accountability mechanisms in Flemish education. They also provide input on whether and how standardised tests may complement these.
- Lessons from the OECD case study (Chapter 7): This maps out the key points identified in the OECD case study against the research-based framework. In doing so, it provides some lessons for the further development of the standardised tests.

References

Janssen, R. et al. (2017), *Validering van IDP en de OVSG-toets : Eindrapport*, Final report on validation of the IDP and OVSG tests, KU Leuven, https://data-onderwijs.vlaanderen.be/documenten/bestand.ashx?id=7760. [7]

OECD (2020), *PISA 2018 Results (Volume V): Effective Policies, Successful Schools*, PISA, OECD Publishing, Paris, https://dx.doi.org/10.1787/ca768d40-en. [6]

OECD (2016), *PISA 2015 Results (Volume II): Policies and Practices for Successful Schools*, PISA, OECD Publishing, Paris, https://dx.doi.org/10.1787/9789264267510-en. [1]

OECD (2015), *Education at a Glance 2015: OECD Indicators*, OECD Publishing, Paris, https://dx.doi.org/10.1787/eag-2015-en. [2]

OECD (2010), *PISA 2009 Results: What Makes a School Successful?: Resources, Policies and Practices (Volume IV)*, PISA, OECD Publishing, Paris, https://dx.doi.org/10.1787/9789264091559-en. [3]

Penninckx, M. et al. (2017), *Zicht op leerwinst. Scenario's voor gestandaardiseerd toetsen (Scenarios for standardised tests)*, Acco, Leuven. [5]

Shewbridge, C. et al. (2011), *OECD Reviews of Evaluation and Assessment in Education: School Evaluation in the Flemish Community of Belgium 2011*, OECD Reviews of Evaluation and Assessment in Education, OECD Publishing, Paris, https://dx.doi.org/10.1787/9789264116726-en. [4]

2 Strategic education governance and case study methods

This Chapter presents a brief overview of the analytical underpinning for the strategic education governance case study and the methods used.

Strategic education governance

The OECD case study is anchored in the strategic education governance analytical framework (Figure 2.1). This draws on a body of work by the Centre for Educational Research and Innovation (CERI) that included research and case studies documenting the complexity of modern education systems and providing insights to evidence on effective governance processes. It is published in two main volumes Burns and Köster (2016[1]) and Burns, Köster and Fuster (2016[2]).

The complexity of education systems arises from the multitude of different stakeholders involved and their various interactions. This stems from a desire to enable greater responsiveness to diverse local demands, multi-level governance arrangements and an increasing number of interactions and activities taking place across different organisational layers. Authorities are joined by parents and other stakeholders in education decision making. Nevertheless, Ministries of education remain responsible for ensuring high quality, efficient, equitable and innovative education at the national level.

With the multitude of stakeholders comes a complex mix of varying perspectives on challenges, differing interpretations of reality and preferred solutions. Information is now more widely gathered than ever before, and while the growing availability of information allows new insights and approaches to shape education, it also prompts new demands and uncertainties.

OECD research identified six interdependent domains of strategic education governance to help government authorities manage the dynamism and complexity of today's education systems while steering a clear course towards established goals (Figure 2.1).

Figure 2.1. Domains of strategic education governance

Accountability
- Enabling local discretion while limiting fragmentation
- Promoting a culture of learning and improvement

Capacity
- Ensuring capacity for policy-making and implementation
- Stimulating horizontal capacity building

Knowledge governance
- Promoting production of adequate evidence
- Mobilising produced evidence for convenient use
- Stimulating a culture of evidence-use
- Nurturing evidence-related capabilities

Stakeholder involvement
- Integrating stakeholder knowledge and perspectives
- Fostering support, shared responsibility, ownership and trust

Strategic thinking
- Crafting, sharing and consolidating a system vision
- Adapting to changing contexts and new knowledge
- Balancing short-term and long-term priorities

Whole-of-system perspective
- Overcoming system inertia
- Developing synergies within the system and moderating tensions

Note: Drawing on the CERI body of knowledge on effective governance processes in complex education systems.
Source: Shewbridge and Köster (2019[3]), *Strategic education governance - Project Plan and Organisational Framework*, http://www.oecd.org/education/ceri/SEG-Project-Plan-org-framework.pdf.

Case study methods

The Flemish Department of Education and Training (the Department) invited the OECD strategic education governance team to conduct a case study on the introduction of standardised tests in Flemish schools. Stakeholder involvement is a central element of the strategic education governance framework and the Department recognised the importance to gather feedback from stakeholders on their perspectives, expectations and motivations. A core ambition of the case study, therefore, is to give insight to stakeholder concerns. That information can guide and help the process of introducing standardised tests. To this end, the case study included three main components:

1. Individual structured discussions with stakeholders (data collection). The OECD team liaised with the Department to obtain contact details for key stakeholders. The OECD team was responsible for contacting stakeholders with an invitation to a structured discussion in English. The invitation included a quick overview of the OECD strategic education governance framework with key points for the discussion (Box 2.1). Stakeholders were not required to prepare for the discussion, but had an idea of how the discussion would be structured and the main vocabulary to be used. Each discussion was scheduled for an hour and lasted a maximum of 80 minutes (depending on the number of participants). In total, fourteen structured discussions were held (Table 2.1). All stakeholders were invited to submit written material and evidence to support their perspectives.

Table 2.1. OECD case study individual structured discussions with stakeholders

In February and March 2021

Stakeholder group	Representative body	Acronym	Invitation accepted
Umbrella organisations	Catholic Education Flanders	KOV	Yes
	Flemish Community education	GO!	Yes
	Educational Secretariat of Flemish Cities and Municipalities	OVSG	Yes
	Flemish Provincial Education	POV	Yes
	Consultation body of small education providers	OKO	Yes
Students	Flemish Student Association	VSK	Yes
Parents	Parent association Flemish Community education	GO!	No reply
	Flemish group of parents and parent associations	VCOV	Yes
	Parent associations from official education	KOOGO	Written feedback
Teacher unions	Socialist teachers' union	ACOD	No reply
	Liberal teacher's union	VSOA	No reply
	Christian teachers' union	COC	Yes
	Christian teachers' union for primary education	COV	No reply
Official bodies	Education Inspectorate		Yes
	Agency for Higher Education, Adult Education, Qualifications and Study Grants	AHOVOKS	Yes
	Department of Education and Training	DOV	Yes
	Agency for Education Services	AGODI	Yes
	Ministerial Cabinet		Yes
Academic experts	Johan Van Braak	UGent	No reply
	Jan Vanhoof	UAntwerpen	Yes

Note: Each interview lasted 60-80 minutes. All interviewees were also invited to submit written material. Follow up invitations were sent to stakeholders who had not replied to offer different time slots for discussions or at a time of their convenience.

> **Box 2.1. Standard text in the OECD team's invitation letters to stakeholders**
>
> We work at the Centre for Educational Research and Innovation within the OECD. Drawing on seven years of research on effective governance in complex education systems, the OECD developed a framework for strategic education governance. This aims to help policy makers and stakeholders apply the OECD's accumulated knowledge and to shine the light on processes that support and sustain effective change.
>
> The Flemish Department of Education and Training has asked us to conduct a case study on the introduction of standardised tests. Applying the OECD principles of strategic education governance, we would like to learn from you how standardised tests could best support your efforts to ensure high quality education for pupils. To familiarise you with our approach, we provide a brief overview of the framework and some of the related considerations for the introduction of standardised tests in Flanders.
>
> **Accountability** provides reasons to other stakeholders for one's actions and the actions of one's organisation. Behind this stands a legitimation purpose, which relates to complying with existing laws and regulations on the one hand, and accounting for the quality and efficiency of education on the other. Accountability can provide recognition of efforts towards providing high quality education. Accountability is central to public trust in the functioning of the education system.
>
> In what ways could standardised tests best contribute to this?
>
> **Capacity** refers to the skills, resources and other enabling factors to carry out tasks and responsibilities. This includes individual skills and organisational structures, including allocating the requisite time and other resources to do so. In schools, important areas include the capacity to collect and analyse a breadth of evidence. This includes existing tests delivered by specific networks, the central tests (*peilingen* and *paralleltoets*), as well as evidence of learning progress via formative assessment and student portfolios; within the network, capacity includes developing tests available to schools and supporting the appropriate use of the results.
>
> What will be the implications of the introduction of standardised tests? What are the opportunities to build on existing capacity? Will there be specific needs for the standardised tests?
>
> **Knowledge governance** seeks to make relevant knowledge available and promote its use. This includes putting in place feedback channels, for instance, for schools and school boards to achieve their goals and engage in quality assurance. Feedback can support accountability to the public as well as school quality assurance processes. A core focus is on fostering adequate capability, opportunity and motivation of key stakeholders (teachers, school leaders, pedagogical advisory services, Flemish Department of Education) to make use of evidence for improving the quality of student learning.
>
> What opportunities could the standardised tests bring for your work? How could you best use the results of standardised tests?
>
> **Stakeholder involvement** integrates the perspectives and knowledge of schools, school boards, networks and other stakeholders in policy making. In Flanders, this safeguards the constitutional principle of freedom of education while creating suitable feedback channels and strengthening accountability to parents and the public. It also helps to identify capacity needs and address concerns, which may otherwise be overlooked.
>
> How can your professional knowledge and expertise contribute to the introduction of standardised tests? What concerns do you have regarding the introduction of standardised tests?
>
> **Strategic thinking** links knowing where to go with strategies of how to get there – especially when contexts change. With evidence from the sample-based assessments *peilingen* and international

> assessments, there is a shared concern among stakeholders on the overall quality of education provided to Flemish pupils. Attainment targets provide 'anchors' to help advance educational efforts towards agreed goals for students.
>
> How could standardised tests best complement the attainment targets as a central 'anchor'? What would be the role of standardised tests in advancing Flanders towards a common goal of educational excellence?
>
> **A whole-of-system perspective** enables a look at the "big picture" of education in Flanders. It supports better learning and efficiency for stakeholders within the system through greater alignment and co-ordination of efforts. In this way, it seeks to maximise synergies and minimise the duplication/waste of time and effort of those involved.
>
> How could the introduction of standardised tests be most efficient for your work? How would you align these with existing quality assurance efforts?

2. Initial reporting of feedback from individual structured discussions with stakeholders (data feedback). The OECD team gave feedback to representatives of the ministerial cabinet on 29 March 2021 regarding stakeholder perceptions of their involvement at early stages in the development of standardised tests (see Chapter 3). The OECD team presented key points of the discussions with stakeholder representatives during the first meeting of the High-level forum on 12 May 2021. The High-level forum was established as a mechanism for feedback and information flow between stakeholders regarding the introduction of standardised tests.

3. Stakeholder reflection seminar on 9 June 2021 (data feedback and collection). This seminar was organised to provide feedback to stakeholders and to challenge them to think about their roles in the introduction and use of the standardised tests. Invitations were organised by the Department, extended to all stakeholders that had been invited to individual discussions with the OECD team in February and March, plus to researchers involved with the university centre and representatives from the Flemish strategic advisory council for education and training (VLOR). In addition, the OECD team had requested that each umbrella organisation invite some school leaders to join the seminar. The OECD team presented its analysis of feedback from stakeholder discussions in February and March. Participants were assigned to four working groups, each with a moderator and note taker from the Department. The working language was Dutch. Each working group discussed two questions:

   - What opportunities do the standardised tests bring for you?
   - What do you need to prepare to get the most out of them in June 2024?

   The note takers sent key points to the OECD team to allow a presentation of a summary overview from working groups (in English).

In total, 36 people participated in the stakeholder reflection seminar. This included representatives from all umbrella organisations, the inspectorate, AGODI, AHOVOKS, the ministerial cabinet, academics from Gent University, Leuven Catholic University, Antwerp University and Vrije Universiteit Brussels, and parent associations and trade unions. The OECD team regretted that due to the timing of the seminar, student representatives were not able to attend. However, the OECD team received written feedback from the Flemish Student Association (VSK) on the two questions that are included in this report. It was grateful for the active participation of all representatives and to gain feedback via the working groups from the trade union (ACOD), parent association (KOOGO) and a range of researchers with whom it had not had the opportunity to discuss in February and March.

References

Burns, T. and F. Köster (eds.) (2016), *Governing Education in a Complex World*, Educational Research and Innovation, OECD Publishing, Paris, https://dx.doi.org/10.1787/9789264255364-en. [1]

Burns, T., F. Köster and M. Fuster (2016), *Education Governance in Action: Lessons from Case Studies*, Educational Research and Innovation, OECD Publishing, Paris, https://dx.doi.org/10.1787/9789264262829-en. [2]

Shewbridge, C. and F. Köster (2019), *Strategic education governance - Project Plan and Organisational Framework*, http://www.oecd.org/education/ceri/SEG-Project-Plan-org-framework.pdf. [3]

3 Stakeholder involvement

Stakeholder involvement can support better policy outcomes and implementation and generate credibility and trust. There is a strong tradition of stakeholder involvement in Flemish education. As an example, the OECD case study was designed to gather feedback from stakeholders on various aspects of the introduction of standardised tests. This chapter includes their perceptions of the mechanisms and consultations for stakeholder involvement during the initial stages and their motivations for involvement.

Stakeholder involvement as a cornerstone of strategic education governance

Central to this OECD case study is the involvement of stakeholders. The Flemish Department for Education and Training (the Department) engaged the OECD team to consult with different stakeholder groups and give each an opportunity to express their perspectives on the introduction of standardised tests. The aim of this consultation being to document different voices and views.

Stakeholder involvement is a cornerstone of the strategic education governance framework (Chapter 2). This recognises that the main benefits of involving stakeholders more directly in the policy-making process are as follows (Burns, Köster and Fuster, 2016[1]):

- Better policy outcomes: ensuring that policies are in line with the needs and interests of stakeholders, while including their knowledge and expertise, can make a policy more fit-for-purpose.
- Better implementation: giving the opportunity to influence the stakes of a policy and simultaneously enhancing the understanding of the policy can raise legitimacy and create ownership by stakeholders.
- Greater trust: providing direct contact and dialogues between policy makers and stakeholders can generate credibility and trust.

An earlier OECD study on the role of the Flemish attainment targets in systemic quality assurance identified the need for continuous dialogue to share different interpretations of the policy, to point to the original aims and background, and to jointly develop new understandings and solutions (Rouw R., 2016[2]).

OECD research on governance in complex education systems points to four elements that support effective stakeholder involvement:

- Clear and active communication and transparency: Stakeholder engagement is based on clear and active communication, ideally tailor-made to a diversity of audiences, and particularly reaching out to the most relevant stakeholders (Burns, Köster and Fuster, 2016[1]). For stakeholders who are not so knowledgeable in policy-making processes, it needs to be clear where decision making happens and how and where they can participate and hold other actors accountable. Transparency entails gathering data and providing stakeholders with information about inputs, processes, outputs and outcomes to prepare their effective participation.
- Careful selection: Identifying and selecting stakeholders can be done for participation in different stages of the policy process. In complex systems, this has become particularly challenging since the number of groups with stakes in education has multiplied. Seeking for a broad and inclusive engagement arena is preferable, but may result in the voice of key stakeholders being diluted. Balancing openness with the recognition of the value of key stakeholders requires a sensible and transparent approach (Rouw R., 2016[2]).
- Capacity building: Different stakeholders require capacity to assume roles and deliver on responsibilities. In many instances, capacity cannot be taken for granted, but needs to be invested on and built deliberately (Burns, Köster and Fuster, 2016[1]). Capacity building also includes developing the competences for participating in stakeholder engagement processes.
- Facilitative leadership: Leadership to engage stakeholders requires facilitative skills and attitudes. Facilitative leadership contributes to empower and mobilise stakeholders, to create trust, to promote consensus and to move collaboration forward, a facilitative leadership. The engaging leader or facilitator is sometimes depicted as a steward, focused on the process, with a high "technical credibility" (Ansell and Gash, 2007[3]).

Chapter 2 provides details of the stakeholders invited to participate in the OECD case study. In Figure 3.1, the OECD team provides an overview diagram presenting key elements related to standardised tests and how these and the various stakeholder groups surround Flemish schools. Central bodies interviewed include the Flemish education inspectorate (the Inspectorate), the Agency for educational services (AGODI) and the Agency for higher education, adult education, qualifications and study grants (AHOVOKS). Stakeholder representative bodies are indicated in blue, as although at the central level, they represent the perspectives of students, teachers and parents.

Figure 3.1. OECD mapping of stakeholders and key elements related to standardised tests

A snapshot of stakeholders invited to participate in the OECD case study

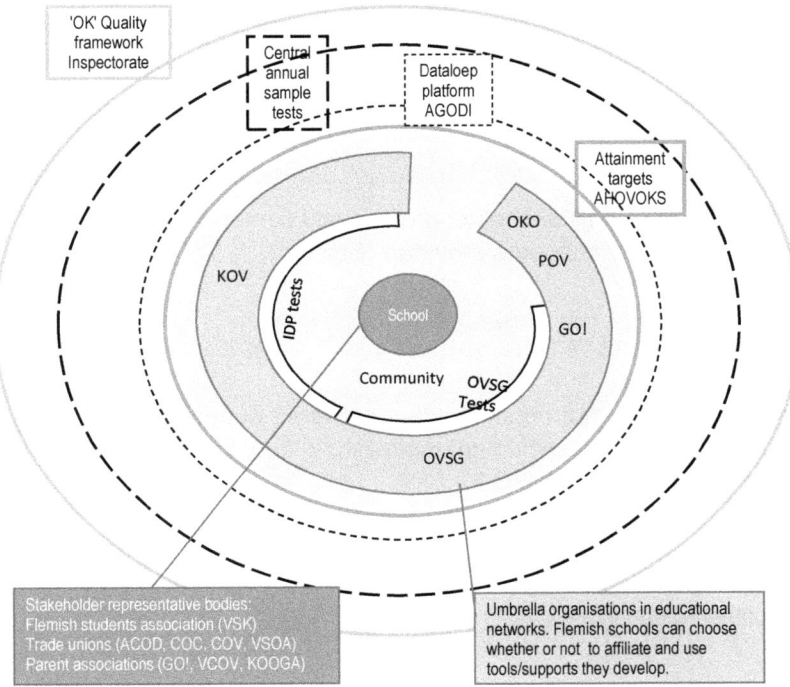

Note: The key elements identified are (from the outside in): the 'OK' Quality framework is a common reference for the inspectorate, umbrella organisations and schools; the central annual sample (*peilingen*) tests students in primary and secondary education; the Dataloep platform provides data feedback to schools; the central attainment targets are set for students in primary and secondary education; and the umbrella organisations Catholic Education Flanders (KOV) and the Educational secretariat of Flemish cities and municipalities (OVSG) offer tests to primary schools. IDP stands for the inter-Diocesan tests offered by KOV.

> **Box 3.1. Discussions with stakeholders on their involvement**
>
> **Stakeholder involvement**
>
> Stakeholder involvement integrates the perspectives and knowledge of schools, school boards, networks and other stakeholders in policy making. In Flanders, this safeguards the constitutional principle of freedom of education while creating suitable feedback channels and strengthening accountability to parents and the public. It also helps to identify capacity needs and address concerns, which may be overlooked otherwise.
>
> - What concerns do you have regarding the introduction of standardised tests?
> - Are you satisfied with your involvement with the introduction of standardised tests?
> - How can your professional knowledge and expertise contribute to the introduction of standardised tests?

The OECD team explored how each stakeholder group could contribute to the introduction of standardised tests and invited them to raise any concerns they had (Box 3.1).

Stakeholder involvement at the initial stages to develop standardised tests

This chapter documents feedback from stakeholders gathered during the OECD case study. As such, it represents the various perceptions, including motivations and concerns, at the initial stages of the development of standardised tests (Figure 3.2).

Figure 3.2. Timeline of initial stakeholder involvement

Situating the feedback gathered during the OECD case study

2020				2021					
Sep.	Oct.	Nov.	Dec.	Jan.	Feb.	Mar.	Apr.	May	June
Feasibility study								Feasibility study release	
SG (18/09)		SG (17/11)	SG (15/12)	SG (19/01)					
			University centre						
					SG (05/02)	SG (25/03)			
				VLOR position statement (21/01)	OECD structured discussions			First high-level forum (12/05)	OECD stakeholder seminar (09/06)

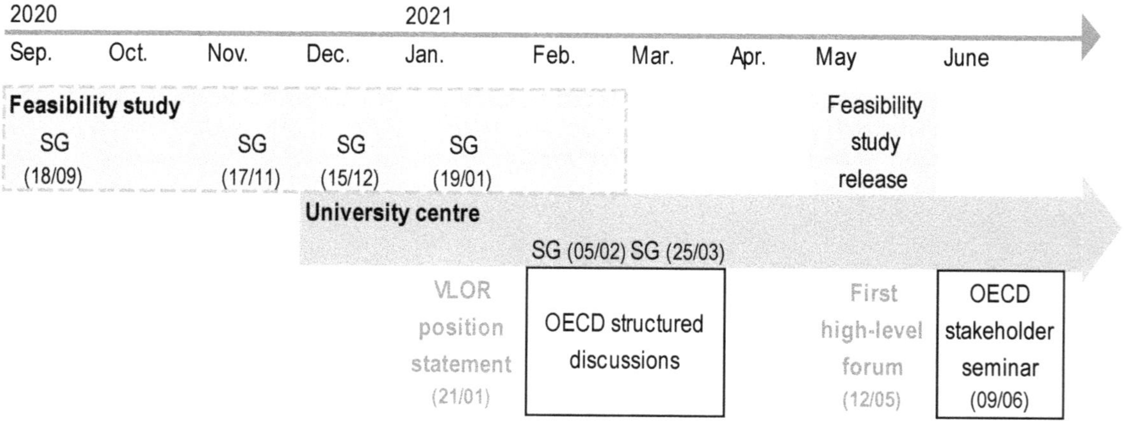

Note: VLOR is the Dutch acronym for the Flemish strategic advisory council for education and training. "The Department" is the Flemish Department of Education and Training. 'SG' stands for steering group.

In the last quarter of 2020, the Department of Education and Training (the Department) had established two main mechanisms to support the development of the standardised tests:

- The **university centre** is a consortium of higher education institutions cooperating with the Department on introducing standardised tests. Their main tasks consist of developing the test items, statistical analyses, designing the feedback and developing scripts for the test administration. The University centre comprises all five universities and two higher education colleges (with teacher training facilities) in Flanders.
- A **steering group** will steer the work of the university centre. The steering group comprises representatives of the Department, the Education Inspectorate, the education providers/umbrella organisations, the education trade unions and the Flemish students association.

On their own initiative, the Flemish strategic advisory council for education and training (VLOR) created a *working group* to give advice on the implementation of standardised tests in Flanders. The VLOR works independently of the Minister and the Department and can provide advice or organise consultations on all educational matters for which the Flemish Community is competent. In January 2021, the VLOR published a text highlighting its concerns and advice on the conditions necessary for the implementation of the standardised tests.

The Minister decided to establish a specific stakeholder consultation platform to facilitate communication and feedback at key stages of the development of standardised tests. The first meeting of this "High-level forum" was convened in May 2021.

- The **high-level forum** is mandated to supervise the key decisions in policy development for introducing the standardised tests. It is a forum for feedback and input from stakeholders regarding all the policy aspects. These include timing, communication, which students will participate in the tests, etc. At the meetings of the forum, stakeholders are given information on recent policy developments.

Stakeholder perceptions of their involvement at the initial stages

Broad support for the early focus on scientific expertise for test development

During discussions with the OECD team, nobody contested the need for scientific experts to play a prominent role in the early stages of development. On the contrary, stakeholders expect scientific rigour and perceive the high reliability and quality of standardised tests as their added value. In support of this, the existing central sample tests (*peilingen*) were often cited and in some discussions also international assessments. The OECD noted a perception that many existing tests used in schools were not of the desired quality. Notably, parental and student representatives raised several doubts and concerns about inconsistencies and varying quality of existing tests used in schools. Many stakeholders referred to evidence from the Inspectorate that supports this (see also Chapter 5).

The university centre unites academic partners from different backgrounds (psychometrics, statistics, Dutch language, mathematics, teacher education) and different institutions to support the development of standardised tests. This is symbolically important in achieving broad academic representation and is a clear strength for the development at early stages, even though individual academic staff may take a more critical stance towards the introduction of standardised tests. In addition, representatives from the Department advise that schools traditionally find it easier to engage with academic actors in joining new initiatives compared to engaging with government actors directly.

Stakeholders voice strong criticism of the initial process

During discussions with the OECD team, with the exception of one interview, stakeholders were strongly critical of the initial process around the introduction of standardised tests. Some took time to describe to the OECD team the regular way of policy making in Flanders (a 'democratic way') and illustrated how the process around the introduction of standardised tests had thus far strongly deviated from that. Some stakeholders also pointed out that while there was no specific legal requirement for stakeholder consultation regarding the setting up of the university centre to develop standardised tests, the established culture in the educational field had been to consult with stakeholders at early stages of policy development.

The VLOR depicts the typical education policy cycle in Flanders, as:

> *The Minister prepares a decree in collaboration with the cabinet and the Department. At that stage, the Minister seeks advice, for example, from the Ministry of Finance and the VLOR. The parliament (decree) and the government (implementing decrees) then decide exactly what the policy measure will look like. This is followed by implementation in the educational field, with the cooperation of the Department and other educational organisations. The inspectorate, feedback from schools, networks and other organisations form an evaluation of the policy, which very often results in the preparation of new policy measures.*

Given this context and widely communicated view on Flemish education policy-making tradition, the OECD team noted that the initial approach to develop standardised tests had left many stakeholders with the perception that they were not involved in the project. Several stakeholders expressed frustration at a lack of consultation opportunities and specifically referenced the OECD case study as a significant step to increase stakeholder involvement.

Motivation for greater and more structured involvement

During all discussions with stakeholders, the OECD team enjoyed open and constructive exchanges. Each stakeholder communicated clear motivations and visions for how the standardised tests would best serve educational improvement. Nobody contested that there was democratic legitimacy for the introduction of standardised tests. This was included in the political manifesto of the current government. Several stakeholders specifically mentioned the legitimacy for the government to require more objective information in an area of significant public investment. Many stakeholders were enthused by the prospect of the availability of reliable and regular data on student outcomes.

The OECD team had discussions with stakeholders before the high-level forum was established. At that time, they were missing a consultation mechanism that would provide more structured feedback. During the majority of discussions with the OECD team, stakeholders referred to the fact that the VLOR had taken the initiative to issue a position statement on the introduction of standardised tests. The implication was that this had happened in the vacuum created by a lack of consultation with stakeholders and their frustration at a lack of official involvement at initial stages. However, the OECD team also noted in some discussions that the process to reach agreement on the VLOR statement had not been easy. Students voiced an inherent tension that the VLOR had issued a position statement while at the same time many of the same stakeholders were involved in the steering group to support the work of the university centre.

During discussions with the OECD team, stakeholders communicated their ideas of how they could have greater involvement in the introduction of standardised tests:

- Network representatives expressed motivation to capitalise on their established relationships with schools and support the integration of standardised tests in schools' self-evaluation processes. One network voiced surprise that the government had not already approached them to build capacity and support in the field.
- Parental representatives appreciate when the government makes direct contact with them and underlined the possibility to design and circulate surveys to their members. This can get timely

feedback to policy makers. They cited the example of quick-turnaround surveys during the ongoing health crisis.
- Student representatives noted the possibility to send a questionnaire to their members to get feedback on student attitudes and expectations on the use of standardised tests.

The OECD team did not have the opportunity to speak with school leader representatives. Going forward their involvement will be critical in defining expectations and support for the use of standardised tests in schools. The pedagogical advisory services (PBD) of umbrella organisations have close contact and good relationships with many school leaders. For example, the OECD team noted that the umbrella organisation Flemish Provincial Education (POV) is prioritising the engagement of school leaders in preparing for standardised tests.

The stakeholder reflection seminar pursued these motivations further, asking participants to think about how they would use the standardised tests and the necessary preparations to ensure their effective introduction and use in Flemish schools. Stakeholder feedback during the seminar echoed and expanded on many of the above points. Chapter 5 presents a summary overview.

Unclear communication from the government on the purpose(s) of standardised tests

Without doubt, the biggest concern raised by stakeholders during discussion with the OECD team was a lack of clarity in communication about the purpose of the standardised tests. Stakeholders reported that there had been confusing and contradictory messages from the government on expectations for how results would be used. It was thought that a narrative on the purpose of the standardised tests was missing and in its absence, speculation and confusion were growing. Below are some examples of the way this was expressed during discussions with the OECD team:

> *"Use of results is entirely missing in government communication at the moment. It is not adequate to simply obtain and give results, there is a need to do something with them."*

> *"There are mixed communications that school rankings are not wanted, but at the same time there is political expectation for results at the school level. Obviously this is incompatible. There is no clarity on how tests will be used."*

> *"There is no framework on the impact of tests for schools, teachers and networks. Much fear is due to a lack of vision on what to do with the tests."*

> *"From the perspective of the educational field, communicating standardised tests as 'a revolution', but without an idea of how, makes this all more delicate and complex."*

These points were echoed in the stakeholder reflection seminar (see Chapter 5). There was an expectation that the different scenarios that had been developed would bring forward a decision on the major purpose(s) of the new standardised tests. Many stakeholders were eager for this clarity so as to better engage with the necessary preparations for developing and working with the standardised tests.

Developments in stakeholder involvement

Policy development and implementation of the standardised tests are ongoing. Since, its direct consultation with stakeholders, the OECD team notes several developments in how the Department is working to involve stakeholders.

- **Communication initiatives**: In June, the Department included an interview of two experts in the teacher magazine (*Klasse*) and organised an online seminar where school leaders could submit their questions and concerns.

- **Working groups with the university centre**: In autumn 2021, the university centre invited teachers, school leaders and representatives of the pedagogical advisory services to participate in working groups. The groups are organised around three topics: (1) the selection of the attainment targets that the standardised tests will cover, (2) test adaptations for students with special educational needs and (3) content and format of the feedback of results to schools. Participation rates in these groups are high, and stakeholders indicate their motivation to participate and to discuss the policy development.
- **Second high-level forum**: By the end of September 2021, the high-level forum received a preparatory text with proposals, based on the feasibility study.

The OECD team notes that the VLOR issued a second position statement in September 2021. In this statement, the VLOR lists several concerns on the introduction of the standardised tests. Their main plea is for a public debate on the standardised tests.

References

Ansell, C. and A. Gash (2007), "Collaborative Governance in Theory and Practice", *Journal of Public Administration Research and Theory*, Vol. 18/4, pp. 543-571, http://dx.doi.org/10.1093/jopart/mum032. [3]

Burns, T., F. Köster and M. Fuster (2016), *Education Governance in Action*, OECD, http://dx.doi.org/10.1787/9789264262829-en. [1]

Rouw R., M. (2016), "United in Diversity: A Complexity Perspective on the Role of Attainment Targets in Quality Assurance in Flanders", *OECD Education Working Papers*, Organisation for Economic Co-Operation and Development (OECD), http://dx.doi.org/10.1787/5jlrb8ftvqs1-en. [2]

4 Strategic thinking and whole-of-system perspective

Strategic thinking requires an approach to policy development that emphasises adaptive capacity and co-operation among stakeholders. It looks to establish shared goals and co-ordinate action. Taking a step back, the OECD team asked stakeholders to think about the Flemish system as a whole. Is there a shared concern on the quality of education? If so, how could standardised tests play a role in addressing this?

Strategic thinking and whole-of-system perspective

Education systems are complex structures with dynamic relationships between stakeholders and decision makers at various levels. Education governance needs to juggle this dynamism and complexity at the same time as steering a clear course towards common goals. To this end, it increasingly relies on strategic thinking (Burns, Köster and Fuster, 2016[1]; Burns and Köster, 2016[2]). This is in line with a growing literature arguing that strategic planning, in the sense of a deliberate, precise and integrated long-term plan, is unsuited in complex environments (Van der Steen and Van Twist, 2018[3]). In education governance, strategic thinking differs from strategic planning in two key ways.

First, it emphasises flexibility and adaptive capacity, rather than being a matter of developing a long-term plan that assumes linear and predictable developments of the system. This is important because addressing complex issues requires being able to respond to varying local conditions and needs, as well as being aware of and prepared for potentially diverging and even unexpected effects of policy interventions (Frankowski et al., 2018[4]).

Second, it is a collaborative process aiming to strengthen capacity for strategic thinking at all decision-making levels of the system, rather than being a matter of the central level or individual decision makers rolling out a plan on all other levels of the system. Policy and reform require simultaneous and sustained interventions at as many parts of the system as possible (Mason, 2008[5]). Effective governance therefore needs to emphasise collaborative dynamics between different parts of the system. It has to build on strategic thinking, collaboration and trust – in contrast to supervision and control, which have been traditional forms of governance in many systems (Osborne, 2006[6]).

New policies have greater potential to succeed if stakeholders share the goals and components of reforms, and take action in alignment with them (Burns, Köster and Fuster, 2016[1]). Introducing new ways of thinking and working together can be difficult in education governance, because existing education systems cannot be turned off, redesigned and restarted. Change therefore needs to be introduced in an iterative manner, even if the change itself is contradictory to current practice (OECD, 2017[7]). New approaches and ways of thinking need to be learnt by doing and their implementation has to be inclusive (Hynes, Lees and Müller, 2020[8]).

The OECD strategic education governance framework conceptualises strategic thinking in education governance as broadly involving three main processes that influence each other:

- Develop common goals: in order to balance short-term priorities with common goals, decision makers need to first develop long-term goals that incorporate various perspectives of stakeholders across the system.
- Adapt to changing contexts: decision makers need to adapt strategies as contexts change and new knowledge emerges from a broad range of sources.
- Co-ordinate action: decision makers need to co-ordinate action and balance tensions by fostering co-operation among stakeholders and education actors, who may have different short-term priorities and work realities.

The OECD team asked each stakeholder group to take a step back and think about the introduction of standardised tests at the macro level. First, is there a shared understanding in Flanders that there is a need to focus more on educational quality and its improvement? If so, what role could standardised tests play towards achieving this? Second, how could standardised tests best align with and complement existing efforts, such as the attainment targets and the 'quality triangle' approach outlining responsibilities for schools, pedagogical advisory services and the inspectorate? This macro perspective fits within the strategic education governance framework in the domains of 'strategic thinking' and 'whole-of-system perspective' (Box 4.1).

> **Box 4.1. Discussions with stakeholders on strategic thinking and whole-of-system perspective**
>
> **Strategic thinking**
>
> Strategic thinking links knowing where to go with strategies of how to get there – especially when contexts change. With evidence from the national sample survey (*peilingen*) and international assessments, there is a shared concern among stakeholders on the overall quality of education provided to Flemish pupils. Attainment targets provide 'anchors' to help advance educational efforts towards agreed goals for students.
>
> - Is our understanding correct that there is 'shared concern' on the overall quality of Flemish education?
> - What would be the role of standardised tests in advancing Flanders towards a common goal of educational excellence?
> - How could standardised tests best complement the attainment targets as a central 'anchor'?
>
> **Whole-of-system perspective**
>
> Taking a whole-of-system perspective enables a look at the "big picture" of education in Flanders. It supports better learning and efficiency for stakeholders within the system through greater alignment and co-ordination of efforts. In this way, it seeks to maximise synergies and minimise the duplication/waste of time and effort of those involved.
>
> - How would standardised tests best align with existing quality assurance efforts?
> - How could the introduction of standardised tests be most efficient for your work?

A shared concern on the overall quality of education in Flanders

During discussions with the OECD team, all stakeholders agreed that there is a shared concern on the overall quality of education. There is high awareness and debate about this in the educational field. This greater awareness has been supported, among other ways, by the collective conferences on the results from the national sample surveys (*peilingen*). This multi-stakeholder discussion engages participants in debate and raises the profile of national results. Given their alignment to the attainment targets, the results of the *peilingen* have driven the debate forward with authority in the educational field. All stakeholders spoke with respect for the 'scientific rigour' of the national sample survey. Alongside cyclical results from participation in international assessments, specifically the OECD's Programme for International Student Assessment (PISA) and the IEA's Progress in International Reading Literacy Study (PIRLS) and Trends in International Mathematics and Science Study (TIMSS), this has augmented the evidence base at the system level.

The OECD team did not note any contradiction or contesting of an observed phenomenon of overall decline in student performance in Flanders. As communicated by several stakeholders 'the diagnosis is there'. However, some stakeholders raised the point that the results from national and international assessments do not reflect the full range of educational quality.

Evidence of performance in primary education

Certainly, results from the national sample assessments (*peilingen*) at Grade 6 indicate significant proportions of Flemish students who do not demonstrate that they have obtained the expected attainment targets (Figure 4.1). Looking at different content areas in mathematics, in 2016 sometimes only 50% or fewer students were found to meet the attainment targets (see left chart in Figure 4.1). In all but one content area, the percentage of students demonstrating that they met the attainment targets had declined since the national assessment in 2009. The national sample assessments in reading comprehension indicate more stability in the proportion of students demonstrating they meet the attainment targets (see right chart in Figure 4.1). However, the most recent assessment in 2018 indicates a decline. Evidence from the international assessment PIRLS indicates a significant decline in the average reading performance of Flemish Grade 6 students between the 2006 (547 points) and 2016 (525 points) assessments (Mullis et al., 2017[9]). Flemish students also sat the PIRLS test in June 2021 and results will be published in December 2022. This will provide another indicator to assess the performance trend.

Figure 4.1. Primary education: evidence from national sample assessments

Percentage of students assessed in Grade 6 who obtained the attainment target in the specified learning area

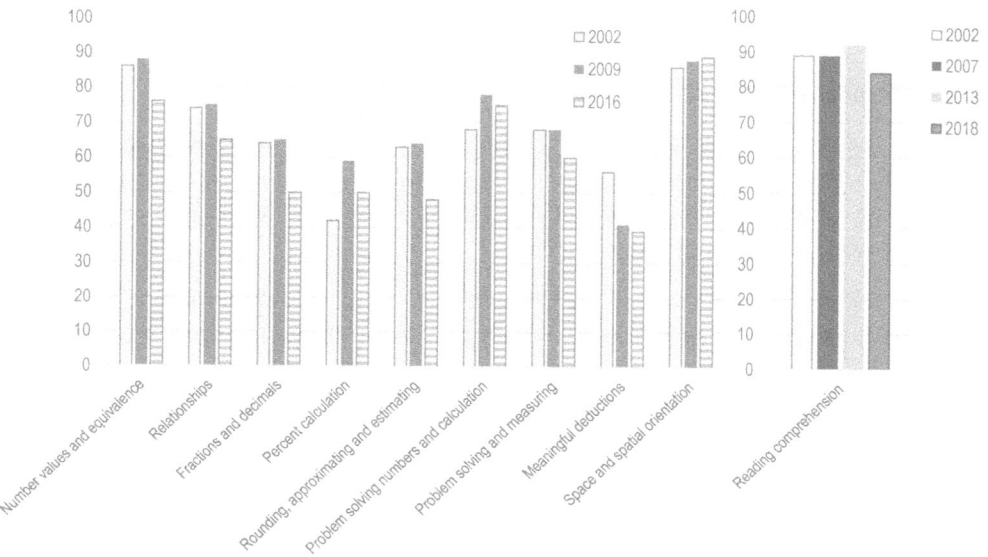

Source: Compiled from data available at Steunpunt Toetsontwikkeling en Peilingen (Steering Group for Development of the Sample Tests) (www.peilingsonderzoek.be).

There is an observed decline in the average performance of Flemish students in the TIMSS international assessments of mathematics and science in Grade 4 (Table 4.1). The observed decline is starkest between the more recent assessments in 2019 and 2015.

It is notable that the observed decline in reading, mathematics and science is across the entire performance distribution, that is, from students who are able to complete the most difficult tasks to students who are able to complete the easiest tasks (Table 4.2). However, it is most significant in the middle of the performance distribution (students who are able to perform on the international benchmarks 'high' or intermediate').

Table 4.1. Primary education: changes in average performance in international assessments

Flemish student performance in the Trends in International Mathematics and Science Study (TIMSS Grade 4)

	Mathematics: average	2019 average compared to reference year	Science: average	2019 average compared to reference year
2019	532		501	
2015	546	**-13**	512	**-10**
2011	549	**-17**	509	**-8**
2003	551	**-18**	518	**-17**

Note: Data in bold denotes a statistically significant difference.
Source: (Mullis et al., 2020[10]).

Table 4.2. Primary education: changes in performance distribution in international assessments

Percentage of students performing at each of the international benchmarks (TIMSS Grade 4, PIRLS Grade 4)

Benchmark	Mathematics		Science		Reading	
	2019	Compared to 2003	2019	Compared to 2003	2016	Compared to 2006
Advanced	8	**-2**	2	0	4	**-3**
High	40	**-11**	24	**-4**	35	**-14**
Intermediate	80	**-10**	66	**-13**	80	**-10**
Low	97	**-2**	92	**-6**	97	**-2**

Note: Data in bold denotes a statistically significant difference. TIMSS is the Trends in International Mathematics and Science Study; PIRLS is the Progress in International Reading Literacy Study.
Source: (Mullis et al., 2020[10]; Mullis et al., 2017[9]).

Table 4.3. Primary education: performance in different content areas of international assessments

Relative strengths and weaknesses of Flemish students (TIMSS Grade 4)

	Percentage of items in overall test	2019 average performance	2019 relative performance in content or cognitive area (compared to Flemish average)	Change in average performance since 2011
Mathematics:		532		
Numbers	50%	526	**-6**	**-25**
Measurement and geometry	30%	551	**18**	-1
Data	20%	527	-6	**-10**
Knowing	40%	546	**14**	**-18**
Applying	40%	526	**-6**	**-19**
Reasoning	20%	530	-2	-1
Science:		501		
Life science	45%	500	-1	**-10**
Physical science	35%	502	1	-5
Earth science	20%	496	-5	**-8**
Knowing	40%	493	**-8**	**-14**
Applying	40%	501	0	**-10**
Reasoning	20%	511	**10**	3

Note: Data in bold denotes a statistically significant difference. TIMSS is the Trends in International Mathematics and Science Study.
Source: (Mullis et al., 2020[10]).

A more fine-grained look into the areas assessed in the international assessments reveals that the observed decline is in the content areas numbers and data for mathematics and in life science and earth science for science (Table 4.3). Flemish students had a high average performance in test items assessing measurement and geometry. In both the mathematics and science assessments, Flemish students' performance declined in test items that assessed the cognitive processes 'knowing' (covering the facts, concepts and procedures students need to know) and 'applying' (focusing on students' ability to apply knowledge and conceptual understanding to solve problems or answer questions). In the science assessment, Flemish students performed relatively better on test items assessing 'reasoning', where students need to go beyond the solution of familiar problems that may have been routinely practiced in lessons to encompass unfamiliar situations, complex contexts, and multistep problems (Mullis et al., 2020[10]).

Evidence of performance in secondary education

Evidence from the national sample assessment, similar to what has been observed in primary education, reveals high proportions of Flemish students in Grade 8 are not able to demonstrate they have obtained the expected attainment targets in various content areas (Figure 4.2).

Figure 4.2. Secondary education: evidence from national sample assessments at Grade 8

Percentage of students assessed who obtained the attainment target in the specified learning area

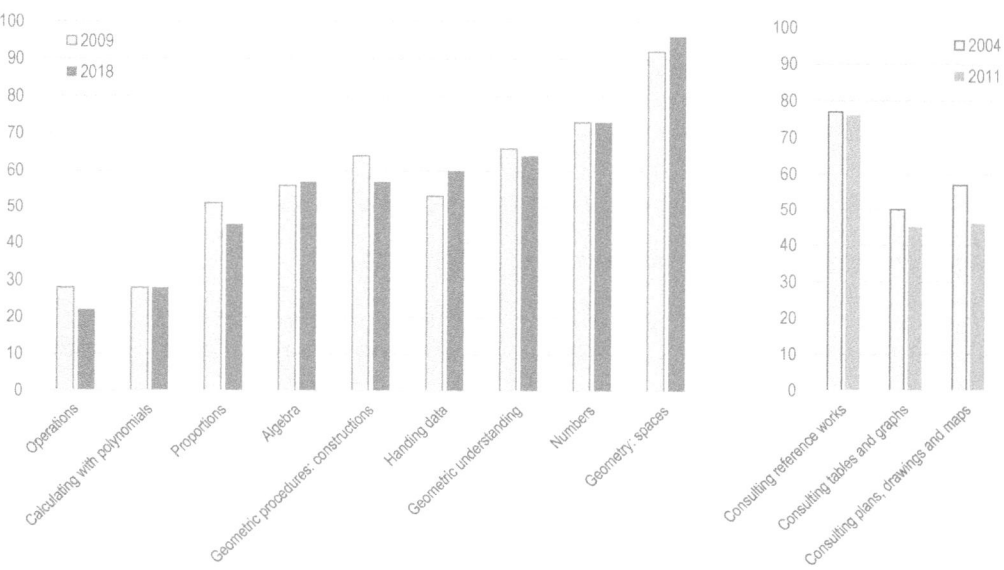

Note: Results are for students in the general stream of education ('A-stroom').
Source: Compiled from data available at *Steunpunt Toetsontwikkeling en Peilingen* (Steering Group for Development of the Sample Tests) (www.peilingsonderzoek.be).

In 2018, this was the case for over 50 per cent of the Flemish students assessed in the mathematical content areas of operations, calculating with polynomials and proportions and there had been no improvement since the equivalent assessment in 2009 (see left chart in Figure 4.2). Also, the national assessments of information processing in 2011 reveal over 50 per cent of Flemish students in Grade 8 did not demonstrate the expected minimum levels in consulting tables, graphs, plans, drawings and maps and that this had declined since 2004 (see right chart in Figure 4.2). For the majority of content areas in Figure 4.2, there is no notable improvement, with the exception of data handling and geometry spaces.

Figure 4.3. Secondary education: evidence from the OECD's PISA (students aged 15)

Mean performance for participating Flemish students (PISA scale score)

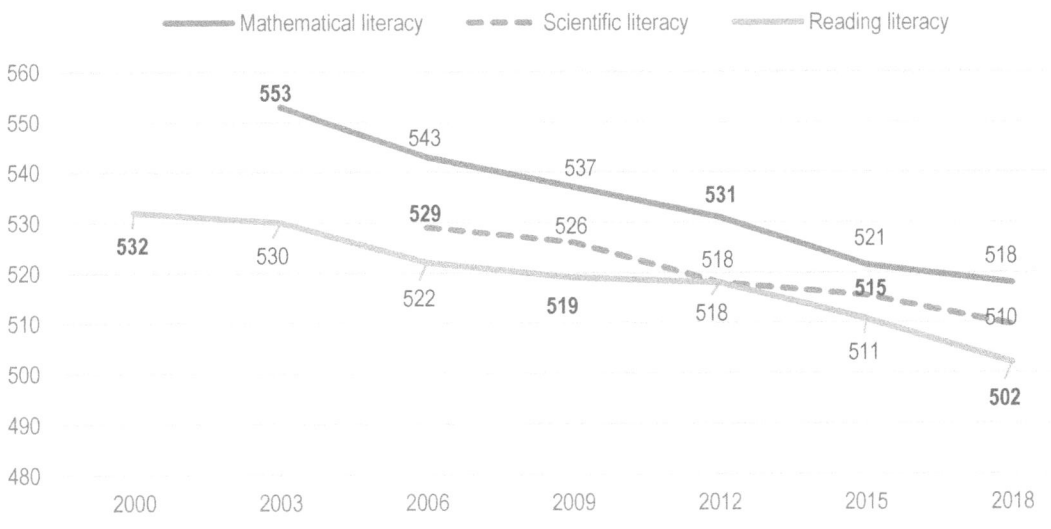

Note: Data displayed in bold indicate statistical significance. For example, for reading literacy the differences in mean performance between 2000 (532), 2009 (519) and 2018 (502) are statistically significant.

Evidence of Flemish grade 8 students' performance in the International Civics and Citizenship Education Study (ICCS) is more encouraging. There is a significant improvement between 2009 (514 points) and 2016 (537 points) (Schulz et al., 2018[11]). The average age of participating students was nearly 14 years old (13.9). The OECD's PISA assesses students at age 15, meaning that students can be in different grades. In PISA 2018, 72% of participating students were in Grade 10, 23% in Grade 9, 4% in Grade 8 and 1% in Grade 11 (OECD, 2020[12]). Evidence from PISA indicates decline in the Flemish students' average performance across the various cycles (Figure 4.3). In each assessment, students complete test items to assess reading, mathematics and science. However, the main focus of each assessment rotates, meaning it is possible to compare performance on a larger set of test items in each of the domains every nine years. In reading, there has been a steady decline in the average performance of Flemish students (between 2000 and 2009 and again between 2009 and 2018). The same is observed for mathematics between 2003 and 2012 and for science between 2006 and 2015. In all areas, the decline over the latter period (between 2015 and 2018) is not statistically significant (OECD, 2019[13]).

A complex debate on educational quality and concerns for equity

During discussions with the OECD team, all stakeholders highlighted that there is a lively debate and many differing opinions/approaches to understanding the reasons behind the observed overall performance decline in Flanders. Most frequently cited points about the broader policy environment relating to quality include: attracting and retaining excellent teachers, teacher education and continued professional development; and different contexts and provision for schools in terms of student composition. When stakeholders referred to differing student composition across schools, they made arguments related to fairness and the need for adequate contextual understanding to interpret results on educational outcomes in a meaningful way.

Compared internationally, both novice and experienced teachers in Flanders report high levels of satisfaction with their salaries, which is an important factor in the attractiveness of the profession (OECD, 2020[14]). In both primary and secondary education, statutory and actual salaries for teachers, particularly upper secondary teachers, in Flanders are above both the OECD and European Union averages (OECD, 2021[15]). This commitment to teacher salaries is reflected in comparatively greater expenditure on education in Flanders: expenditure on educational institutions per full-time equivalent student in 2018 was USD 13 507 in Flanders, compared to an OECD average of USD 10 454 (OECD, 2021[15]). As in other OECD countries, teacher salaries in Flanders remain less competitive than those for other similarly educated workers, but are most competitive at the upper secondary level (OECD, 2021[15]).

However, there is also international evidence to back up the concerns raised on attracting and retaining excellent teachers. First, the perceived attractiveness of the teaching profession has declined in Flanders over recent years (Table 4.4). Notably, between the TALIS 2013 and 2018 surveys more Flemish lower secondary teachers agree that they wonder whether it would have been better to choose another profession and less agree that the advantages of being a teacher clearly outweigh the disadvantages. Along with this, there was a significant decrease in the percentages of lower secondary teachers and school leaders agreeing that the teaching profession is valued in society. Second, reports on stress levels and negative impacts on mental health are also above the OECD average (Table 4.4).

Table 4.4. Feedback from educators on the prestige of the teaching profession and stress levels

Teacher and school leader reports in TALIS 2018 and 2013

Percentages agreeing or strongly agreeing that:	Flanders	OECD
"The teaching profession is valued in society"		
- Primary teachers	30.8	n.a.
- Lower secondary teachers	25.8	25.8
Change in reports by lower secondary teachers since TALIS 2013	-20.1	n.a.
- Lower secondary school leaders	43.9	36.9
Change in reports by lower secondary school leaders since TALIS 2013	-15.0	n.a.
"The advantages of being a teacher clearly outweigh the disadvantages"		
- Lower secondary teachers	70.2	76.0
- Change since TALIS 2013	-14.4	n.a.
"I wonder whether it would have been better to choose another profession"		
- Lower secondary education teachers	30.0	33.8
- Change since TALIS 2013	+7.3	n.a.
"My job negatively impacts my mental health"		
- Primary teachers	32.8	n.a.
- Lower secondary teachers	32.5	23.7
"I experience stress in my work" (answer 'quite a bit' or 'a lot')		
- Primary teachers	72.5	n.a.
- Lower secondary teachers	69.1	48.7

Source: Compiled from data in (OECD, 2020[14]).

Third, there is evidence of staff shortages gathered from Flemish school leaders as part of the PISA 2018 survey. Compared to the OECD average, there are reportedly higher proportions of Flemish teachers working part time and while the percentage of fully certified teachers compares favourably, there are higher proportions of Flemish students in schools with a reported lack of teaching staff or inadequate or poorly qualified teaching staff (Table 4.5). There is also a concern for equity with the percentage of fully certified teachers reportedly lower in socio-economically disadvantaged schools.

Table 4.5. Secondary education: feedback from school leaders on staff qualification and shortages

Based on reports from school leaders in participating schools (PISA 2018)

	Flanders	OECD average
Percentage of fully certified teachers	87.0	81.8
- in socio-economically advantaged schools	93.1	82.8
- in socio-economically disadvantaged schools	85.4	80.3
Percentage of full-time teachers	76.6	86.6
Percentage of part-time teachers	23.4	13.4
Percentage of students in schools where instruction is hindered due to:		
- A lack of teaching staff	31.6	27.1
- A lack of assisting staff	24.0	32.8
- Inadequate or poorly qualified teaching staff	21.6	15.6
- Inadequate or poorly qualified assisting staff	14.1	16.5

Source: Compiled from data in (OECD, 2020[12]).

Figure 4.4. Secondary education: feedback from school leaders on school admission policies

Percentage of PISA students in schools where the school leader reported these admission policies

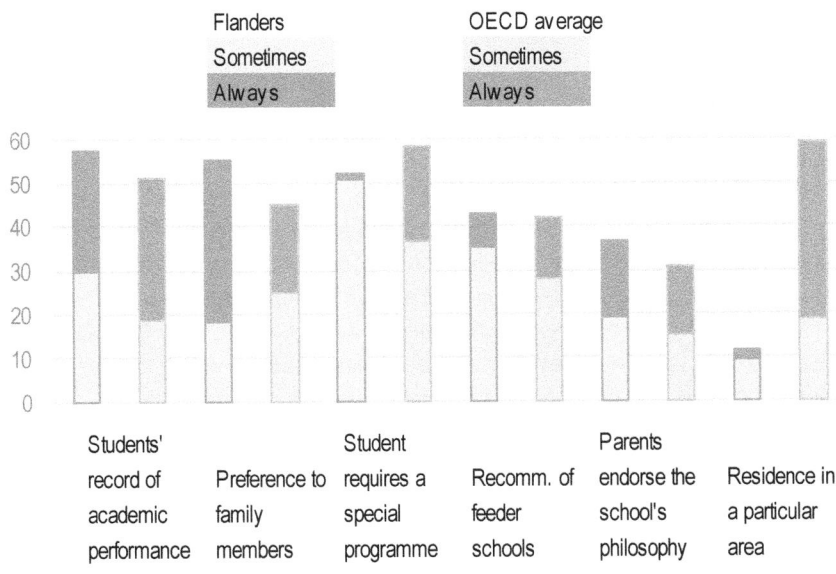

Source: Compiled from data in (OECD, 2020[12]).

During discussions with the OECD team, stakeholders also noted the importance of the strategic goal to reduce inequities in Flemish education. In consideration of this, many stakeholders voiced great sensitivity about the possibility of the results of standardised tests being available to the broader public. Various stakeholders pointed to the highly competitive context within the Flemish education system and raised strong concerns about the potential use of results by the media to publish simplistic and misleading rankings of school performance. Several stakeholders specifically raised the need to find a legal basis to prevent such 'misuse'.

To illustrate the competitive context and the minimal tradition of making information on schools public, stakeholders contributed several anecdotal points. These included: initial anxiety in the education field regarding the publication of inspection reports for individual schools and attempts by the media to sensationalise these; the failure of multi-stakeholder equal opportunity platforms (*Lokaal OverlegPlatform*) to make concrete agreements on student intake; some schools relying heavily on early streaming/tracking of students; and middle class parents paying for people to camp outside certain schools to enrol their children.

The Belgian constitution guarantees freedom of education, including the freedom to choose a school and even to establish a school. Data from PISA 2018 reflect this, revealing that Flemish students have a greater choice of secondary schools in their area, compared to their international counterparts (83% have at least two or more schools in the area, compared to 63% on average in the OECD) (OECD, 2020[12]). In contrast to the OECD average, Flemish school leaders report that residence in a particular area is not a very widespread criterion in admitting students to school (Figure 4.4). Much more commonplace are students' academic performance and/or interest in a special programme, which is largely explained by the tracking in Flemish secondary education and the fact that many schools offer only one or two tracks. In theory, schools (both primary and secondary) cannot refuse students based on their academic performance. Students in Flanders get priority admission when an older brother or sister attends the school or when one of the parents is a member of staff. This latter policy reportedly plays a more important role in Flemish secondary education compared to on average in the OECD. These results are striking in how admission policies may differ among Flemish schools and lend support to concerns raised by parents and students of a highly competitive context.

Support for standardised tests as tools for school development

The OECD noted from the different discussions with stakeholders a coherent expectation on the role that standardised tests could play in advancing Flemish education towards educational excellence. Standardised tests would be a tool for schools, providing regular, reliable student test results in two key areas. The standardised nature would give all Flemish schools access to objective and comparable feedback. The expectation is that the availability of such data would stimulate schools to focus on outcomes and further strengthen the culture of quality assurance at the school level. The OECD team attributes the coherence of this in part to the fact that several stakeholders made explicit reference to the Flemish Education Council (VLOR) position statement on conditions for high quality tests:

> *Their potential added value lies in a development-oriented use of the tests. Under the right conditions, the information from tests can support schools to take responsibility for developing their own educational quality.*

The OECD team notes that this may also be influenced by an awareness of previous research testing out different scenarios for the development and use of standardised tests in Flanders (Penninckx et al., 2017[16]).

The major argument made for introducing standardised tests primarily as a tool for school quality development was the need to gain trust in the educational field. During several discussions, the OECD team noted enthusiasm to capitalise on and nurture the openness to embrace the opportunities that standardised tests would bring. The OECD team heard that, in general, attitudes regarding the potential usefulness of standardised tests had evolved over recent years and noted a sense that this was a pivotal moment. However, stakeholders also underlined that this openness was by no means universal and that there is a need to build trust through concrete experiences in schools. Notably, the teacher union representatives during discussions with the OECD team commented that they are yet to be convinced of the real value that standardised tests would bring to teachers and schools and raised the challenge of whether it would be better to invest resources in professional development and capacity building.

According to reports in the TALIS 2018 survey, the majority of Flemish teachers and school leaders view their colleagues as open to change and their schools as places that have the capacity to adopt innovative practices. However, this is not the case in all Flemish schools and, in particular, openness to change and accepting new ideas in lower secondary education is low by international comparison, as reported by both teachers and school leaders (Figure 4.5). Among the OECD countries with available data, primary teachers are more open to change, but the differences are 'particularly pronounced' in Flanders between primary and lower secondary teachers (OECD, 2019[17]).

Figure 4.5. Openness to change: feedback from teachers and school leaders

Percentage of teachers or school leaders agreeing or strongly agreeing with the specified statements (TALIS 2018)

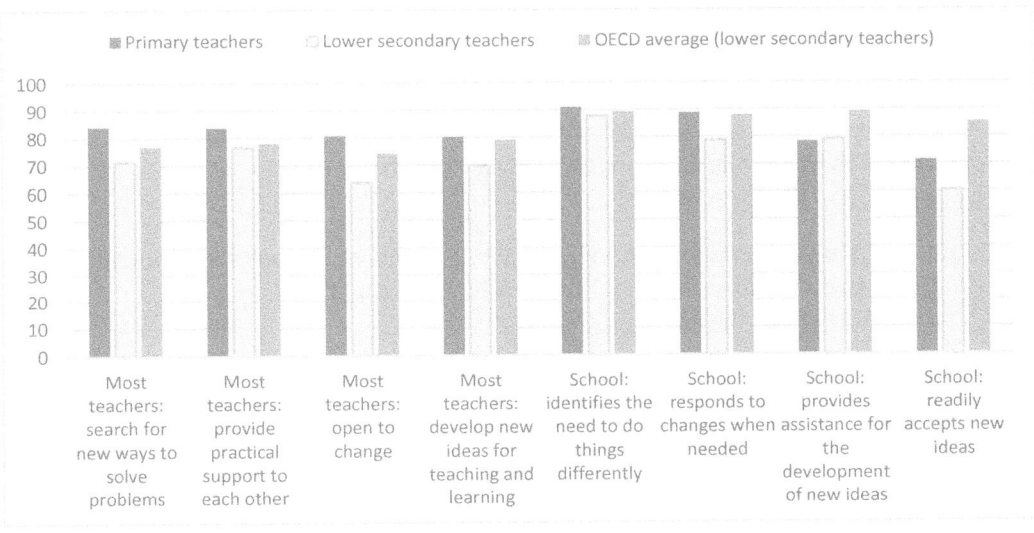

Note: The first four points are reported by teachers ("Most teachers in the school..."); the last four points are reported by school leaders ("The school quickly..."). There is no OECD average for primary teachers as not all OECD countries chose to administer the survey at this level.
Source: Compiled from data in (OECD, 2019[17]).

In Chapter 5, the OECD team presents an overview of the various motivations cited by different stakeholders during the stakeholder reflection seminar. During discussions with the OECD team, several stakeholders made specific reference to consistent findings from the Inspectorate that point to insufficient focus on goals/outcomes at the school level (for evidence from inspections see Chapter 6). In all discussions with pedagogical advisory services, representatives noted the variation in capacity (and sometimes motivation) among schools and emphasised recent efforts to heighten their focus on supporting schools' quality assurance efforts. They argue that the availability of regular, objective data from the standardised tests would bolster their support efforts (see also Chapter 5).

Student representatives expressed strong support for the role that standardised tests could play in promoting a more rigorous approach to grading in schools and within networks. They raised prominent concerns regarding current assessment practices and the reliability of many tests used in schools. According to reports from Flemish lower secondary teachers, there is not an established culture to work with other teachers in school to ensure common standards in student evaluations (22% of Flemish lower secondary teachers reported this in TALIS 2018, compared to 40% on average in the OECD) (OECD,

2020[14]). Although limited to assessing competences in Dutch and mathematics, student representatives expressed their hopes that the introduction of standardised tests would promote a more rigorous approach to grading equivalency at the school level (see also Chapter 5).

References

Burns, T. and F. Köster (eds.) (2016), *Governing Education in a Complex World*, Educational Research and Innovation, OECD Publishing, Paris, https://dx.doi.org/10.1787/9789264255364-en. [2]

Burns, T., F. Köster and M. Fuster (2016), *Education Governance in Action: Lessons from Case Studies*, Educational Research and Innovation, OECD Publishing, Paris, https://dx.doi.org/10.1787/9789264262829-en. [1]

Frankowski, A. et al. (2018), "Dilemmas of central governance and distributed autonomy in education", *OECD Education Working Papers*, No. 189, OECD Publishing, Paris, https://dx.doi.org/10.1787/060260bf-en. [4]

Hynes, W., M. Lees and J. Müller (eds.) (2020), *Systemic Thinking for Policy Making: The Potential of Systems Analysis for Addressing Global Policy Challenges in the 21st Century*, New Approaches to Economic Challenges, OECD Publishing, Paris, https://dx.doi.org/10.1787/879c4f7a-en. [8]

Mason, M. (2008), "What is complexity theory and what are its implications for educational change?", *Educational Philosophy and Theory*, Vol. 40/1, pp. 35-49, http://dx.doi.org/10.1111/j.1469-5812.2007.00413.x. [5]

Mullis, I. et al. (2017), *PIRLS 2016 International Results in Reading*, International Association for the Evaluation of Educational Achievement (IEA), https://files.eric.ed.gov/fulltext/ED580353.pdf. [9]

Mullis, I. et al. (2020), *TIMSS 2019 International Results in Mathematics and Science*, International Association for the Evaluation of Educational Achievement (IEA). [10]

OECD (2021), *Education at a Glance 2021: OECD Indicators*, OECD Publishing, Paris, https://dx.doi.org/10.1787/b35a14e5-en. [15]

OECD (2020), *PISA 2018 Results (Volume V): Effective Policies, Successful Schools*, PISA, OECD Publishing, Paris, https://dx.doi.org/10.1787/ca768d40-en. [12]

OECD (2020), *TALIS 2018 Results (Volume II): Teachers and School Leaders as Valued Professionals*, TALIS, OECD Publishing, Paris, https://dx.doi.org/10.1787/19cf08df-en. [14]

OECD (2019), *PISA 2018 Results (Volume I)*, OECD, http://dx.doi.org/10.1787/5f07c754-en. [13]

OECD (2019), *TALIS 2018 Results (Volume I): Teachers and School Leaders as Lifelong Learners*, TALIS, OECD Publishing, Paris, https://dx.doi.org/10.1787/1d0bc92a-en. [17]

OECD (2017), *Systems Approaches to Public Sector Challenges: Working with Change*, OECD Publishing, Paris, https://dx.doi.org/10.1787/9789264279865-en. [7]

Osborne, S. (2006), "The New Public Governance?", *Public Management Review*, Vol. 8/3, pp. 377-387, http://dx.doi.org/10.1080/14719030600853022. [6]

Penninckx, M. et al. (2017), *Zicht op leerwinst. Scenario's voor gestandaardiseerd toetsen (Scenarios for standardised tests)*, Acco, Leuven. [16]

Schulz, W. et al. (2018), *Becoming Citizens in a Changing World*, Springer International Publishing, Cham, http://dx.doi.org/10.1007/978-3-319-73963-2. [11]

Van der Steen, M. and M. Van Twist (2018), "Strategies for robustness: Five perspectives on how policy design is done", *Policy and Society*, Vol. 37(4), pp. 491-513, https://doi.org/10.1080/14494035.2018.1520782. [3]

5 Capacity and knowledge governance

This chapter presents the results of stakeholder consultations that relate to how prepared the system is to deliver and effectively introduce standardised tests. Using a research-based framework that promotes the systematic use of evidence by decision makers, it notes the importance of not only the availability of data that standardised tests can supply, but more importantly the motivations and capabilities of stakeholders to use these. How do they best see these supporting their efforts to improve student learning?

Capacity

In the OECD strategic education governance framework, the capacity of stakeholders, in terms of time available, resources and skills to take up their roles and responsibilities are of central importance. Such considerations relate to the maturity of the culture and readiness to adopt and integrate new approaches and how diverse this is within the system. With the introduction of standardised tests, the OECD team asked stakeholders to assess how they would integrate these and whether there would be specific needs within the system (Box 5.1).

Box 5.1. Discussions with stakeholders on capacity and knowledge governance

Capacity

Capacity refers to the skills, resources and other enabling factors to carry out tasks and responsibilities. This includes individual skills and organisational structures, including allocating the requisite time and other resources to do so.

In schools, important areas include the capacity to collect and analyse a breadth of evidence. This includes existing tests delivered by specific networks, the national assessments (*peilingen* and *paralleltoetsen*), as well as evidence of learning progress via formative assessment and student portfolios.

Within the network, capacity includes developing tests available to schools and supporting the appropriate use of the results.

- What will be the implications of the introduction of standardised tests?
- What are the opportunities to build on existing capacity?
- Will there be specific needs for using the standardised tests?

Knowledge governance

Knowledge governance seeks to make relevant knowledge available and promote its use. This includes putting in place feedback channels, for instance, for schools and school boards to achieve their goals and engage in quality assurance. Feedback can support accountability to the public as well as school quality assurance processes. A core focus is on fostering adequate capability, opportunity and motivation of key stakeholders (teachers, school leaders, pedagogical advisory services, Flemish department of education) to make use of evidence for improving the quality of student learning.

- What opportunities could the standardised tests bring for your work/learning?
- How could you best use the results of standardised tests?

Capacity for test development, administration and school quality assurance

Existing capacity for test development within the Flemish system

The annual national sample-based tests (*Peilingen*) are developed and scored by the Centre for Test Development and Assessment (Catholic University Leuven and University of Antwerp). These tests are developed each year for the sixth grade of primary education and the second, fourth or sixth grade of full-time secondary education. The Centre also offers a set of parallel tests (*Paralleltoetsen*) for schools that are interested. These are offered as supports for school self-evaluation. The Centre provides guidance on how these should be administered, scores student performance on the tests and provides a feedback report to schools with results. All tests are paper-based, although the Centre has been exploring the feasibility of using a digital platform.

In primary education, schools must ensure that students are tested in the final year (Grade 6) as a support to verify student achievement in at least three learning domains. This requirement was introduced in 2018/19. Schools are free to choose from the government toolkit of validated tests (Table 5.1). The main tests used by schools are those developed by the Catholic Education Flanders (KOV) and Educational Secretariat of Flemish Cities and Municipalities (OVSG) umbrella organisations. Only few schools use the available central parallel tests (*paralleltoetsen*).

During discussions with the OECD team, representatives from both umbrella organisations currently developing validated tests expressed great pride in the high participation rates of schools opting to use tests within their networks. In 2015/16, 85% of KOV schools used its Grade 6 test and 98% of OVSG schools and 92% of the GO! Community schools used the OVSG tests (Janssen et al., 2017[1]). Representatives advised that this has created familiarity with tests and demonstrates high levels of trust in schools for the support provided by their networks. However, representatives from both networks underlined that they have limited resources and capacity for test development and that the 'scientific process' for test development is limited. Limited statistical capacity has consequences for reliability of the tests with respect to the difficulty of tests from year to year and the reporting back to schools on averages, notably for 'comparable school groups' which contextualise the results based on school composition data (Janssen et al., 2017[1]). Professionals take on test development tasks in addition to their other responsibilities and work with groups of volunteers. For OVSG this comprises about twenty pedagogical advisors. For KOV this comprises pedagogical advisors, policy supporters and teacher educators. Representatives advised the OECD team that capacity for test development is roughly around two to three full-time equivalent staff.

Table 5.1. Toolkit of validated tests for use by primary schools

	Central parallel tests (*Paralleltoets*) Centre for Test Development and Assessment (Catholic University Leuven and University of Antwerp)	Catholic Education Flanders (KOV) Inter-diocesan tests (IDP)	Education Secretariat of Cities and Municipalities of the Flemish Community (OVSG)
Grades	6	4 and 6	6
Test administration	May/June	June May (online trial)	June (written) School year (practical)
Learning domain tested	Dutch, Mathematics, French, People and Society, Science and Engineering, Information processing	Dutch, Mathematics, People and Society, Science and Engineering	All-talent test (Dutch, Mathematics, French, World orientation, Artistic education)
Content focus	Attainment targets	Network curriculum	Network curriculum
Mode	Paper-based tests	Paper-based tests Online tests Practical tests	Paper-based tests Practical tests Online tests
Feedback focus	School level	School level	School level Individual students
Benchmark	Standard set by experts for attainment targets (*cesuur*) Adjustments for some student characteristics	Average for Catholic schools Similar context groupings	Average for OVSG schools and for GO! Schools Similar context groupings

Note: Primary schools must administer validated tests for at least three learning domains.
Source: Eurydice; (Janssen et al., 2017[1]).

Expectations for scientific rigour and independence of standardised tests development

The initial mechanisms established by the Department of Education and Training seek to engage a broad range of technical expertise, as embodied in the University Centre, and a multi-stakeholder group to steer the development and administration of the tests. During the discussions with stakeholders, the OECD team noted strong confidence in the scientific expertise in the consortium of the University Centre. There is appreciation for the potential synergies that a consortium of expertise can bring for test development capacity. Stakeholders voiced expectations for scientific rigour and independence of standardised tests.

When introducing new assessments, many countries have chosen to establish specific bodies with responsibilities in this area. A series of reviews of evaluation and assessment in OECD countries pointed to the importance of ensuring adequate system capacity for the design, implementation and reporting and feedback of results in national assessment systems (OECD, 2013[2]). Considerable investment is required to develop capacity and expertise in standardised test development and it takes time to develop the necessary expertise. A central body with specific responsibility for educational assessment can provide technical autonomy from the education authorities with the necessary distance from political decision making. Central capacity, in whatever form, can both symbolise greater focus on the importance of assessment and influence perceptions throughout the system on the reliability of tests used. As the OECD reviews documented, to varying degrees among countries and over different political cycles, there may be different tensions put on national evaluation bodies, including limited resources available for their activities, restructuring and in some cases, closure.

Capacity in schools to administer digital tests

OECD data collected as part of the PISA 2018 survey show Flemish secondary schools in a positive position in terms of perceived school capacity related to digital devices. At least four out of five Flemish students participating in PISA 2018 were in schools whose leader reported sufficient number of digital devices, with connection to the Internet and sufficient bandwidth or speed (Figure 5.1). Two-thirds of students were reportedly in schools with an effective online learning support platform. However, these data indicate that not all secondary school leaders thought digital capacity was sufficient at their school. Note that these reports predate the COVID19 health crisis, which put much greater focus on the use of such platforms. In the spring of 2021, the Flemish government provided schools with extra budget to buy digital devices and to strengthen connectivity. From Grade 5 onwards, schools receive funding to buy a device for every single students. For students in Grade 4 (and below) the school receives a budget to buy computers that students can share.

During some interviews, comments were made regarding the current capacity within Flemish schools to administer digital tests at scale. Parental representatives were doubtful that all schools would be ready to do so. Such concerns need to be addressed with authoritative data on the availability and adequacy of digital resources in Flemish schools. Notably, the umbrella organisation KOV administers some of its tests online and pays attention to capacity with a trial run in May before administering the real tests in June (Table 5.1) In June 2021, 40% of schools participating in the OVSG tests administered these online, as this option was offered for the first time. An OVSG press release points to feedback that barriers for other schools include limited ICT infrastructure, teachers' fear of digital testing and trust in the digital system, but that participating schools will continue to administer online tests (OSVG, 2021[3]). AHOVOKS provided a concrete illustration of varying capacity in schools to run digital tests. Due to the health crisis, the entrance examination to study medicine or dentistry in 2020 had to be organised differently. Instead of being held centrally in Brussels, it was held in several secondary schools and the experience showed that not all schools had the requisite hardware and had to borrow computers to administer the examination. However, these are high stakes examinations for students and so the administration at the same time for all students is an important aspect. Regardless, these points indicate the need to have a careful review and feedback from schools on such points of logistical implementation.

Figure 5.1. School leaders' perceptions of school capacity related to digital devices (DD)

Percentage of students in schools whose school leader agreed or strongly agreed with the following (PISA 2018)

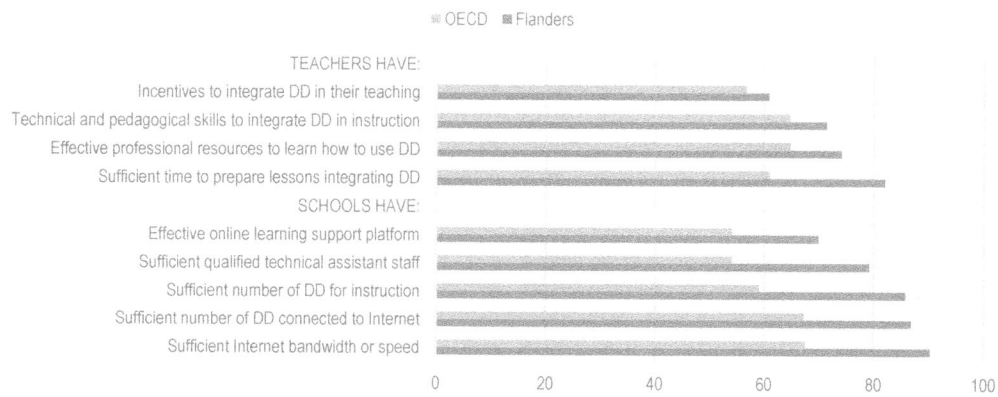

Source: Compiled from data in (OECD, 2020[4])

Evidence from inspections that many schools need to improve self-evaluation

During interviews, many stakeholders referred to the variation in school quality assurance processes. All school network representatives noted this from their work with schools and offer of support and development work within their respective network. Evidence from inspections in Flemish primary and secondary schools back this up and is obviously widely communicated among stakeholders.

Table 5.2. Expectations for school quality assurance capacity in Flemish schools

Criterion	Judgement that the school meets expectations
K1 Vision and strategic policy	The school knows what it wants to achieve with its education, how it wants to shape the school functioning and how it wants to stimulate the development of its pupils. The vision is attuned to the input and context of the school and to the regulations. It is widely and visibly used in school life and teaching practice. The school stimulated the joint responsibility to realise the vision.
K2 Organisation policy	The school develops and implements a policy in which participation and dialogue are important. It is open to external questions and expectations and regularly responds to them. It stimulates innovation, reflection and the sharing of expertise between team members. It works together with others to strengthen teaching practice and school functioning. It communicates frequently, transparently and purposefully about its operations with internal and external stakeholders.
K3 Educational policy	The school develops the quality of its teaching practice. It gives shape to teaching practice and improving professionalism by means of targeted measures and agreements. It supports the team members.
K4 Systematic evaluation of the quality	The school systematically evaluates various aspects of school functioning. It devotes specific attention to the evaluation of teaching practice.
K5 Reliable evaluation of the quality	The school evaluates its quality in a targeted way based on the available qualitative and quantitative sources. It involves relevant partners in its evaluations. It pays specific attention in its evaluations to the results and effects on the pupils. Evaluations are generally reliable.
K6 Secure and adjust	The school has an insight into its strengths and points to work on. It stores and distributes what is of high quality. It develops targeted improvement actions for the points it needs to work on.

Note: For all criteria, schools can also be judged to exceed expectations. There are four possible judgements: below expectations, near expectations, meets expectations and exceeds expectations.
Source: (Onderwijsinspectie, 2019[5]).

The greater focus in the inspection approach on school quality assurance processes provides regular insight to the maturity of the evaluation culture in Flemish schools. Evidence from school inspections conducted in the school years 2018/19 and 2019/20 shows variation in school quality assurance processes at both primary and secondary level. The Quality reference framework includes a set of six criteria that collectively capture and set expectations for a school's capacity to assure its quality (Table 5.2)

Among the six criteria used to evaluate school quality assurance processes, 'K5 Reliable evaluation of the quality' addresses the use of student test results. While serious concerns were identified in only a small number of schools inspected, the reliability of evaluations of school quality was judged to not fully meet expectations in 47.2% of the primary schools and in 37.0% of the secondary schools (Figure 5.2). This means that:

> The school evaluated its quality in a limited and targeted way based on the available qualitative and quantitative sources. It misses out on opportunities to involve the expertise of relevant partners in its evaluations. It does not yet succeed in using the results and effects for the pupils in its evaluations. This puts the reliability of the evaluations at risk (Onderwijsinspectie, 2019).

Reliability here refers to a lack of externality or objectivity in evaluations. It also points out that the school does not make use of the results and does not benefit from the expertise of 'relevant partners', which would include the pedagogical advisory support services available in most networks.

The majority of secondary schools inspected do not fully meet expectations on the criteria 'K4 Systematic evaluation of the quality' and 'K3 Educational policy'. Together these point to fragmented and unsystematic approaches to school evaluation and related improvement actions.

Figure 5.2. Quality assurance capacity in Flemish primary and secondary schools

Data from inspections conducted in school years 2018/19 and 2019/20

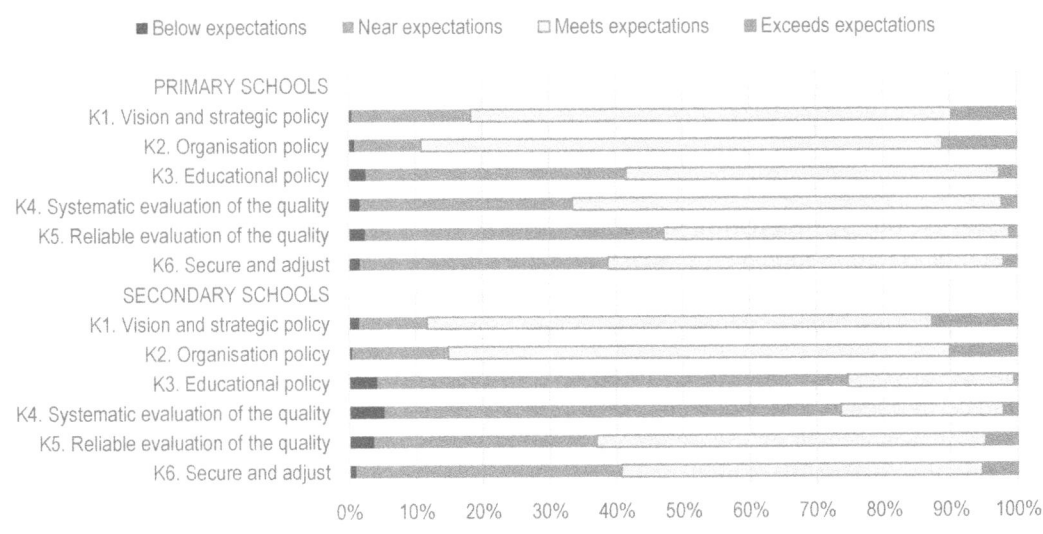

Note: Judgements on six criteria used to inspect quality assurance capacity. Compiled from inspections conducted in 534 primary schools and 189 secondary schools.
Source: data provided by the Flemish Inspectorate.

Time for testing in the school calendar

Student representatives commented that with the introduction of standardised tests there would need to be a review of the overall workload and time commitment for pupils. Concerns were raised in respect to the existing set of tests and whether standardised tests would simply add to these or replace some. The Flemish Student Association (VSK) underlines a concern on current workload for students and a request for greater co-ordination of teacher planning on homework and assessment (VSK, n.d.[6]). Student concerns about a lack of co-ordination are mirrored in the official inspection evaluations finding fragmented practices in many Flemish schools, particularly at the secondary level (Figure 5.2).

The VSK also appeals for less summative assessment (grading, sorting of students into specific groups, etc.). (VSK, n.d.[6]). This is directly linked with the notion of workload, as with higher stakes attached there is more preparation time for students. During the discussion with the OECD team, students reported anecdotally very different approaches to how existing tests (such as *paralleltoetsen*) are used in schools and that some teachers/schools attach stakes to these, which adds test preparation time for students. Data from PISA 2018 reflect the different emphases placed on academic performance and placement tests among Flemish schools, with 28 percent of participating 15-year-olds in schools where such information was always considered for admission to the school and conversely 43% where this was never considered (OECD, 2020[4]). An evaluation of the umbrella organisation tests by KOV and OVSG did not look into how schools administer and use results of tests, but noted that this is an area that would need to be looked into (Janssen et al., 2017[1]).

Knowledge governance: promoting the systematic use of evidence

In the OECD strategic education governance framework, knowledge governance is closely linked with capacity. It goes beyond the supply side of knowledge governance to think about the more comprehensive and complex nature of knowledge and its flow and use within an education system. Clearly, the supply and access to knowledge is an important aspect, but so too are motivations and capabilities of stakeholders to consult and act on it. Taking this comprehensive approach, the OECD uses a research-based framework to promote the use of evidence by educational decision makers (Figure 5.3). This draws on the work of (Langer, Tripney and Gough, 2016[7]) where evidence pertains to the product of any "systematic investigative process employed to increase or revise current knowledge". This includes formal research, for example as carried out by research institutions, government agencies or think tanks; systematically gathered understandings from education practice and the practice of policy making, implementation, and evaluation; as well as factual administrative and achievement data (Langer, Tripney and Gough, 2016[7]). Results from standardised tests constitute one important form of evidence.

Effective knowledge governance addresses three factors that promote the use of evidence in decision making: opportunity, capability and motivation (Figure 5.3). These are based on a theory of behavioural change that identifies opportunity as those factors external to the individual that may prompt a change in behaviour, including the availability of evidence, e.g. in forms of access to a data warehouse or indeed the results of standardised tests, and the time to consult and use the evidence. The two other aspects relate to the individual concerned: capability includes having the necessary knowledge and skills to engage in the activity, and motivation includes analytical decision making, habits and emotional responses (Michie, van Stralen and West, 2011[8]). At the core of this is a recognition that while making different forms of evidence available is a fundamental requirement, this is by no means sufficient to translate to its active use and integration in daily work and practices. It is of equal importance to consider the capabilities and motivations of those involved in the daily work of student learning and the organisational and support processes that surround them.

Figure 5.3. Promoting the systematic use of evidence by decision makers

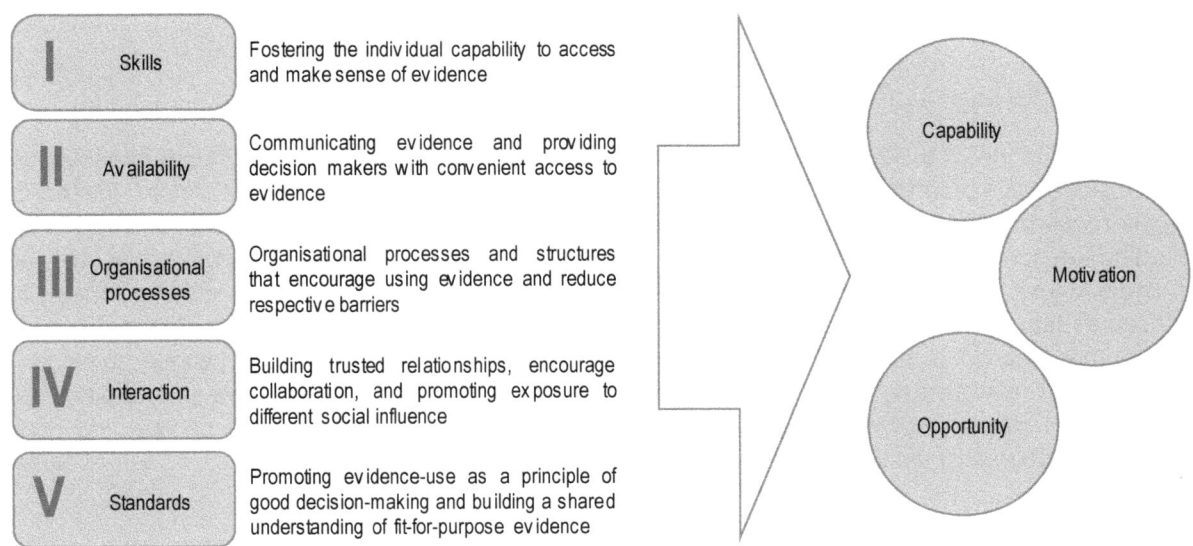

Source: Adapted from (Langer, Tripney and Gough, 2016[7]).

Motivations and capabilities for using the results of standardised tests

Motivations for using standardised tests results

The OECD team asked stakeholders about the opportunities the standardised tests could bring for their work or learning (Box 5.1). This was also the focus of working group discussions in the stakeholder reflection seminar in June (see an overview of key points in Table 5.4).

There is already recognition of the importance of motivation at the school level to data collection within the Flemish system. Drawing on experience with other administrative data collection, representatives from AGODI commented that it is difficult to get good quality data from schools if schools do not see the value in this. Schools are more motivated and engaged when they know why the data are collected and get something in return, learning something from the process. This is entirely in line with the theory of behavioural change at the core of the OECD framework (Figure 5.3). The OECD team did not interview school leader representatives and understanding their motivations will be critical in the further development of standardised tests.

Based on stakeholder feedback, the OECD team identifies the major motivations below.

Reliable information on outcomes for students, teachers and schools

During the discussion with student representatives, the OECD team noted their expectations for "better quality tests with a scientific basis". The greater reliability and objectivity of standardised tests and results was also pointed to by other stakeholders at the reflection seminar, specifically the networks and school leaders (Table 5.4). This echoes previous research to establish different scenarios and investigate social support for introducing standardised tests in Flanders that found strong consensus on the expectation that such tests would contribute to more reliable assessment of students (Penninckx et al., 2017[9]).

Student representatives expressed strong support for the role that standardised tests could play in promoting a more rigorous approach to grading in schools. They raised prominent concerns regarding current assessment practices and the reliability of many tests used in schools. Although the standardised tests would be limited to Dutch and mathematics, there is hope that these would promote a more rigorous approach to grading equivalency at the school level. This was echoed by academics in the stakeholder reflection seminar (Table 5.4).

Comparative feedback to schools for reflection on their development

Certainly, at the network level, discussions with the OECD team highlighted an understanding that standardised tests would bring additional value for schools and school development. Again, this echoes previous research finding stakeholder support for the introduction of standardised tests to support self-evaluation in schools (Penninckx et al., 2017[9]). All network representatives noted that the new standardised tests would provide reliable and comparative feedback to schools. Even if some schools had chosen to administer the existing national tests (*paralleltoets*), the advantage of the new standardised tests would be that all schools would get feedback, providing richer information for the network as a whole. At the stakeholder reflection seminar, network representatives also commented that the standardised tests would allow to rebalance their discussions with schools to include greater focus on learning results (Table 5.4). A degree of external challenge supports the developmental function of school self-evaluation (OECD, 2013[2]).

Among the networks currently developing and administering their own validated tests, representatives from Catholic Education Flanders used the analogy that standardised tests would provide 'a reliable mirror': schools will gain an idea of how they relate to other schools or the expected standard. Similarly, representatives from OVSG agreed that the value of standardised tests would be in pointing out strengths and weaknesses in a comparative light. Also, neither network currently develops or provides tests in secondary education so this is of particular added value to them and their work with schools.

Tools to strengthen and promote a culture of feedback for student learning

Above all, students voiced their major motivation that the new tests would promote greater focus on feedback from teachers ("What to do and how to improve once the results are in?"). Their hope is that the new tests would provide useful feedback for teachers to work on with students and generally stimulate a more feedback-driven culture (Table 5.4). A series of OECD reviews found that teachers in several countries were positive about formative assessments as a tool to help decide the focus of improvement plans for individual students and also for greater collaboration with colleagues. However, the timeliness of results coming back to teachers and the granularity of feedback was critical to their perceived usefulness (OECD, 2013[2]).

Table 5.3. Flemish student perceptions of teacher feedback (PISA 2018)

Percentage of students who reported the following things occur in their language-of-instruction lessons

		Never of almost never	Some lessons	Many lessons	Every lesson or almost every lesson
The teacher gives me feedback on my strengths in this subject	Flanders	33.9	44.0	18.6	3.4
	OECD average	29.5	36.9	23.7	10.0
The teacher tells me in which areas I can still improve	Flanders	27.5	44.9	23.4	4.2
	OECD average	19.8	37.2	30.0	13.0
The teacher tells me how I can improve my performance	Flanders	26.8	45.4	23.2	4.6
	OECD average	18.6	36.8	30.2	14.3

Note: Together these three statements formed the basis of the PISA 2018 index on teacher feedback. For comparison, among OECD countries the average index value was 0.01, with a value of -0.35 in Flanders, ranging from a low of -0.41 in Slovenia to a high of 0.53 in the United Kingdom.
Source: Compiled from data in (OECD, 2019[10])

Information gathered during the PISA 2018 survey reflects that a lack of feedback from teachers is a frustration for Flemish students. In fact, they report the second lowest levels of teacher feedback across OECD countries. This is captured with respect to receiving feedback from their teachers on their strengths and areas for improvement in Dutch language lessons, with a quarter of students reporting that teachers never or almost never give feedback on areas they need to improve and how to do so (Table 5.3).

A recent study looked at the relationship between different aspects reported by teachers and school leaders in TALIS 2018 and the performance of students in PISA 2018 in nine education systems (OECD, 2021[11]). It found a positive relationship between the time teachers reported spending on marking and correcting student work and both student performance and their educational expectations. The researchers note that this may reflect regularity of feedback to students and/or a culture or greater use of testing in higher performing schools. Feedback based on school and classroom results (e.g. performance, results, project results, test scores) was also associated with better performance in the PISA 2018 reading assessment.

Table 5.4. Stakeholder perceptions on opportunities the standardised tests could offer

Feedback from the stakeholder reflection seminar

Stakeholder	Perceived opportunities
Academics	Heighten focus on student outcomes Stimulate teachers to make better tests More direct support from academics to schools Data on student outcomes to support research on what factors make a difference in schools Monitor changes over time at school level Feedback for educational development at school and system levels
Parents	Strengthen focus on quality of education Greater focus on development-oriented change Better feedback and guidance to students
School leaders	Support and strengthen data-driven school policy Support and promote more reliable feedback to students
Networks	Information on educational outcomes at the system level Reliable feedback to schools and networks Advantage that all schools will get feedback (unlike with the *peilingen*) this can strengthen internal quality assurance Rebalance discussions with schools to include greater focus on learning results (often about wellbeing and care) Schools without culture of network support will get feedback for school quality reflection
Teacher Unions	Can augment the evidence base for school quality development Build on experience with using validated tests at the primary level in quality assurance Stimulate professional development in data use
Inspectorate	Augment evidence base for the Inspectorate Support the implementation of a more differentiated inspection approach Support school internal quality control
Students	Better validity of tests (does this test measure what it should?) More reliable testing in and between schools and teachers Use this new instrument to promote a feedback-driven culture Useful feedback for teachers to work on with students Better quality guarantee of diplomas

Note: The Flemish Student Association (VSK) could not attend the seminar, but provided written input on the two questions discussed.

A catalyst to deepen professionals' skills for using evidence and data

Representatives from teacher unions see the introduction of standardised tests as an opportunity to stimulate professional development in data use (Table 5.4). In primary education, this can build on teacher experiences with using the current validated tests. In PISA 2018, Flemish school leaders report comparatively lower participation rates of teachers in professional development programmes (36% of teachers in Flanders had attended a programme in the past 3 months, compared to an OECD average of 53%) (OECD, 2020[4]). A recent OECD study found that the amount of time Flemish teachers spent engaged in continuous professional learning was 'critically low'. The perception of the role of data in relation to teachers' professional learning seemed to be often neutral or even negative, with few schools asking for the results of national tests and many considering that engaging with data remains challenging (OECD, 2021[12]). A small study found little or no systematic use of data in decisions on grade repetition. Among randomly selected first grade primary school teachers, a recent decision on grade repetition was 'largely affected by intuitive expertise and feelings of knowing' (Vanlommel et al., 2017[13]).

Networks with pedagogical advisory services providing support to schools see an opportunity to strengthen their collaborations and work with schools, based on the regular availability of results from standardised tests. During discussions with the OECD team, representatives from all networks underlined the importance of building capacity at the school level to work effectively with the results of standardised tests. They are motivated to mobilise support for schools to develop action plans for improvement, drawing on their established relationships with schools and familiarity with the different contexts. These points were echoed by network representatives in working groups at the stakeholder reflection seminar (Table 5.4). Feedback from Flemish school leaders in the TALIS 2018, in line with their counterparts in other countries, point to data use and teacher collaboration as priority professional development needs. However, the demand is comparatively high in Flemish lower secondary schools: 42% of school leaders report a high need for professional development to develop collaboration among teachers (compared to an average of 24%) and 40% to use data for improving the quality of the school (compared to an average of 26%) (OECD, 2019[14]).

Data for educational research and policy

Discussions with academics and officials underlined the benefit that system-wide information on outcomes would bring for research and policy. There are clear expectations that such information will provide an evidence base for better policy evaluation and inform more effective and efficient policy making. Comparable information for all Flemish schools at different educational levels would also strengthen the focus on the Flemish education system as a whole. At the stakeholder reflection seminar, the point was raised that feedback from the standardised tests could be used to evaluate the attainment targets (Table 5.4).

Regular data to augment the evidence base for school inspections

The Flemish Inspectorate sees the regular school-level data that standardised tests will provide as an opportunity to augment its evidence base for school inspections system wide and also to implement its more differentiated approach (Table 5.4).

Getting ready: thinking of capabilities to make effective use of standardised tests

At the stakeholder reflection seminar, participants were asked to think about and identify necessary preparations to support the effective development, introduction and use of standardised tests, as planned in May 2024. The following points were underlined as necessary to collectively build the engagement and motivation of schools (Table 5.5).

Clarity on purpose(s) of the standardised tests

All stakeholders again repeated their pleas for clarity on the agreed purposes for the standardised tests. Academics require clarity in order to design and develop fit-for-purpose tests. For other stakeholders, their necessary preparations will need to align with the agreed purposes. Several stakeholders reiterated their wish to see the introduction of standardised tests as tools to support school development and to stimulate in earnest a professional culture of evidence use. They expressed the concern that the use of the standardised tests for accountability purposes would undermine their use for school development.

A clear and uniform communication strategy

With these motivations in mind, stakeholders note the need for careful preparations and considerable attention to a communication strategy. Parental representatives call for clear and uniform communication on the nature and appropriate use of results from the standardised tests. Communication should be timely and accessible and address key questions such as:

> *How will the standardised tests improve student learning?*
>
> *Will results of standardised tests provide better guidance?*
>
> *What will change once we have the standardised tests?*

Planning time and adequate resources in schools

Many of the above-mentioned motivations explicitly relate to expectations to improve capabilities at the school level for using data for development. Teacher Union representatives underline the need for careful planning of resources to allow adequate time to both administer standardised tests and analyse and use the results. In preparation for May 2024, paying attention to these planning aspects and allowing the space for educators to build the skills to work with these new tools will enhance their use. In a similar vein, students would wish to see more coherence and planning of student testing, with less reliance on summative tests.

Preparing clear guidance for schools on how to use the results of standardised tests

Academics note the need to prepare explanatory materials on what the standardised tests can and cannot measure and examples of how to place the results in a broader perspective. School networks and the Inspectorate see a role in helping schools interpret the results in a proportionate and informative way for school development. School leaders underline the need for guidance for schools on how to use the results. This is in recognition of the important role they will play in introducing the tests in their schools, working with teachers to clarify the goals of the tests and to note and address any criticisms they may have.

Support and professionalisation of schools and teachers

Academics, the network pedagogical advisory services and the Inspectorate all see a role in supporting schools in using the results of standardised tests for school development. This can build on the established quality framework as a basis to ensure a proportionate and accurate interpretation of the results. The networks can also work with academics to build on their experiences with developing feedback reports for schools and how schools best interpret these in their context. It will be critical to work on the "data literacy" of teachers; otherwise the opportunities the standardised tests offer will be lost.

Table 5.5. Feedback from the stakeholder seminar on necessary preparations

Stakeholder	Necessary preparations for effective implementation and use in June 2024
Academics	Clear and agreed purposes for test design Ensure quality of the test items Avoid pitfalls of inappropriate use of results with reasonable adjustments Further work on how to measure learning gains Solid ICT platform Evaluation of feasibility to make authentic tests with digital platform Communication on what the tests can and cannot capture Place the results in a broader perspective Involvement of all partners (school development) Skills to work with data for school development
Parents	Build trust with clear, accessible, timely and uniform communication to parents from the different channels of communication Clarity on reasonable adjustments for students with specific needs Avoid risks that different schools would attach different weight to the results
School leaders	Guidance for schools on how to use the results Work to clarify the goals of the tests with teachers and to address criticism Professionalisation of schools and teachers to action the results for improvement
Networks	Clarity on whether/how networks will have access to school results while guaranteeing no school reporting to the public Ensure that some accountability at school level does not impede developmental use at teacher and student levels Demonstrate the benefits (compared to *peilingen*) outweigh the costs Enough time and people in networks to support schools Build on existing expertise within networks to support schools with professional development needs related to data use Share current expertise within networks on feedback reports and follow up support and discussions with schools Translate feedback to the curriculum (*leerplan*) and position the results within the broader Quality framework Create the right conditions in schools to use test results and guide schools to work with data more systematically Communication to teachers on associated workload with the tests and added value for school evaluation policy (it is everyone's story, not just teachers whose students sit tests)
Teacher Unions	Clear communication on which scenario will be used for tests Guarantees on the use of data: emphasis on school level (not class level) Build trust/safe environment for teachers Professional autonomy and adequate time for teachers
Inspectorate	Work with guidance on interpreting results (what the tests do and do not show about school quality; what they mean in an educational process; one source of information) Partner with networks to enable differentiated working
Students	An integrated plan for the stimulation of feedback and a focus on the learning process in the classroom A plan and commitment that there will be less summative testing in Flemish schools Avoiding the use of standardised test results for ranking and competition between schools

Note: The Flemish Student Association (VSK) could not attend the seminar, but provided written input on the two questions discussed.

These preparatory points noted by stakeholders collectively recognise the reality of differing existing capacity within the system (see section on Capacity).

References

Janssen, R. et al. (2017), *Validering van IDP en de OVSG-toets : Eindrapport*, Final report on validation of the IDP and OVSG tests, KU Leuven, https://data-onderwijs.vlaanderen.be/documenten/bestand.ashx?id=7760. [1]

Langer, L., J. Tripney and D. Gough (2016), *The Science of Using Science - Researching the Use of Research Evidence in Decision-Making*, EPPI-Centre, Social Science Research Unit, UCL Institute of Education, University College London, http://eppi.ioe.ac.uk/cms/Default. (accessed on 15 January 2018). [7]

Michie, S., M. van Stralen and R. West (2011), "The behaviour change wheel: A new method for characterising and designing behaviour change interventions", *Implementation Science*, Vol. 6/1, http://dx.doi.org/10.1186/1748-5908-6-42. [8]

OECD (2021), *Positive, High-achieving Students?: What Schools and Teachers Can Do*, TALIS, OECD Publishing, Paris, https://dx.doi.org/10.1787/3b9551db-en. [11]

OECD (2021), "Teachers' professional learning study: Diagnostic report for the Flemish Community of Belgium", *OECD Education Policy Perspectives*, No. 31, OECD Publishing, Paris, https://dx.doi.org/10.1787/7a6d6736-en. [12]

OECD (2020), *PISA 2018 Results (Volume V): Effective Policies, Successful Schools*, PISA, OECD Publishing, Paris, https://dx.doi.org/10.1787/ca768d40-en. [4]

OECD (2019), *PISA 2018 Results (Volume III): What School Life Means for Students' Lives*, PISA, OECD Publishing, Paris, https://dx.doi.org/10.1787/acd78851-en. [10]

OECD (2019), *TALIS 2018 Results (Volume I): Teachers and School Leaders as Lifelong Learners*, TALIS, OECD Publishing, Paris, https://dx.doi.org/10.1787/1d0bc92a-en. [14]

OECD (2013), *Synergies for Better Learning: An International Perspective on Evaluation and Assessment*, OECD Reviews of Evaluation and Assessment in Education, OECD Publishing, Paris, https://dx.doi.org/10.1787/9789264190658-en. [2]

Onderwijsinspectie (2019), *Developmental scales for quality development*, http://www.onderwijsinspectie.be. [5]

OSVG (2021), "OVSG-toets kent hoogste aantal deelnemers ooit (OVSG has highest number of participants ever)", *Press Release*, https://www.ovsg.be/pers/ovsg-toets-kent-hoogste-aantal-deelnemers-ooit. [3]

Penninckx, M. et al. (2017), "Delphi study on standardized systems to monitor student learning outcomes in Flanders: mechanisms for building trust and/or control?", *Studia paedagogica*, Vol. 22/2, pp. 9-31, http://dx.doi.org/10.5817/sp2017-2-2. [9]

Vanlommel, K. et al. (2017), "Teachers' decision-making: Data based or intuition driven?", *International Journal of Educational Research*, Vol. 83, pp. 75-83, http://dx.doi.org/10.1016/j.ijer.2017.02.013. [13]

VSK (n.d.), "Kick af van de puntenverslaving (Kick the addiction to grades)", https://www.stemvanscholieren.be/talent-krijgt-alle-kansen. [6]

6 Accountability

Accountability has a legitimacy purpose and supports public trust in the quality of education provided. The information generated and exchanges between the professionals involved can also promote learning. Stakeholders shared their perspectives on school accountability in Flanders and how the standardised tests could contribute to this.

Accountability

Accountability aims to establish public trust in the functioning of the education system. It involves providing reasons to stakeholders and the broader public for one's actions. The purpose is primarily legitimation, as it relates to complying with existing laws and regulations on the one hand, and accounting for the quality and efficiency of the services provided on the other (Rouw et al., 2016[1]; Shewbridge, Fuster and Rouw, 2019[2]).

Importantly, accountability, if designed well, can be an important source of information for feedback, learning and improvement to those involved. To this end, OECD's work on strategic education governance underlines the importance of managing the relational aspects of accountability. Accountability relationships are social processes between those carrying out their work and responsibilities (actors) and those checking this work (forums) against expectations. These exchanges and interactions are the source of learning on both sides of the relationship.

Figure 6.1. Generating learning through constructive accountability relationships

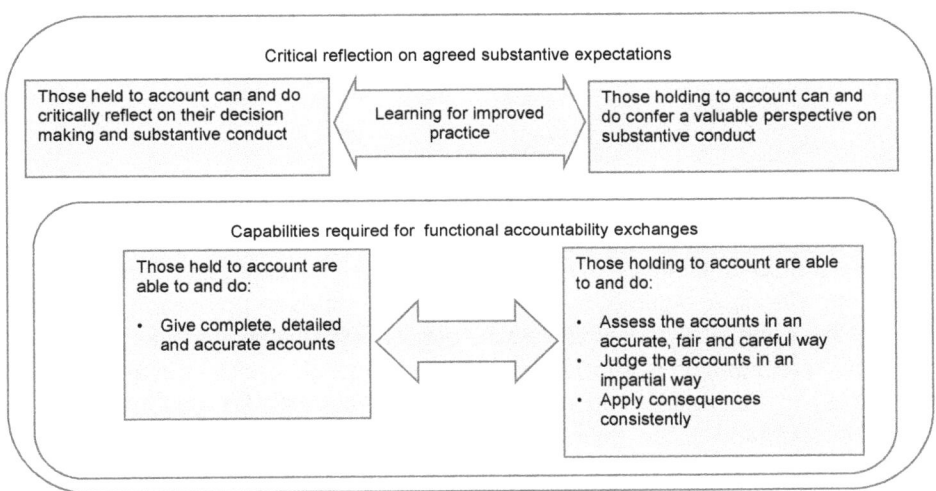

Note: Arrows represent the interactions between those being held to account (actors) on the left and those holding to account (forum) on the right.

There are three key components in a functional accountability exchange (represented in the inner box in Figure 6.1). On one side of the relationship, actors need to give detailed and accurate accounts of their work and decisions over the complete set of demands. On the other side, forums must make an accurate, fair and careful assessment of these accounts and apply in a consistent and fair way their verdict and any potential consequences for actors (Fahey and Köster, 2019[3]). Any functional accountability exchange carries some learning for actors (Schillemans and Smulders, 2015[4]). At the very least, actors can 'learn' whether they achieve expectations of a forum against some measure of performance.

Beyond this, accountability can promote learning by increasing the availability of relevant and accurate information to guide improvement. Accountability relationships can support and motivate actors to learn by reflecting on their past and present conduct with the goal to validate and, where necessary, improve their substantive practice. Actors learn when the forum can provide a valuable perspective on their substantive conduct and its ability to do so grows through repeated interactions with those whose work they assess (represented in the outer box in Figure 6.1).

In designing and/or implementing accountability mechanisms, policy makers should be aware that they will influence the way actors and forums interact with each other and that this can be an important lever for constructive accountability relationships that promote learning. When those involved in accountability exchanges experience meaningful interactions this helps build a record of successful co-operation (which in turn can strengthen credibility and enhance trust), and helps participants to adapt to each other's expectations for the specific relationship with its context, challenges and legacies (Fahey and Köster, 2019[3]; Olsen, 2013[5]; Schillemans and Busuioc, 2014[6]). Ways that policy makers can balance accountability instruments and foster constructive accountability relationships include:

- ensuring the 'fit' of accountability instruments with the existing landscape of organisations, cultures and decision-making traditions
- focusing accountability relationships on what is substantively expected of those who carry out work
- organising the agreement and disagreement over expectations among the varied stakeholders in education governance.

The OECD team explored with each stakeholder group how standardised tests could contribute to accountability in the Flemish education system (Box 6.1). These discussions gave insights to the existing culture and traditions in accountability and allowed the OECD team to document what stakeholders appreciate about this, where they express frustrations and how they think standardised tests could support their efforts going forward.

> **Box 6.1. Discussion with stakeholders on accountability**
>
> **Accountability**
>
> Accountability provides reasons to other stakeholders for one's actions and the actions of one's organisation. Behind this stands a legitimation purpose, which relates to complying with existing laws and regulations on the one hand, and accounting for the quality and efficiency of education on the other. Accountability can provide recognition of efforts towards providing high quality education. Accountability is central to public trust in the functioning of the education system. Beyond accountability for a legitimation purpose, accountability can take a role in stimulating open-minded critical reflection on practice and the use of information gathered in accountability exchanges to improve practice.
>
> - In what ways could standardised tests best contribute to this?

Accountability in Flanders and the introduction of standardised tests

Accountability is understood as a matter of internal responsibility to provide quality education

An important consideration for a functional accountability system is how well it 'fits' with existing organisations, their cultures, and the appropriateness with respect to broader socio-cultural contexts (Stacey, 1995[7]; Lanivich et al., 2010[8]; Gelfand, Lim and Raver, 2004[9]). During all discussions with the OECD team, stakeholders underlined the importance of 'responsibility' as a fundamental concept in Flemish education. Understanding accountability as a matter of internal responsibility to provide quality education is rooted in the comprehensive concept of freedom of education and the central role of autonomous schools and their umbrella organisations in quality assurance (Box 6.2).

In this way, the OECD team noted a broad consensus from stakeholders that standardised tests would best contribute as tools to support schools in their responsibilities. During discussions with the OECD team, many stakeholders took the time to challenge a too narrow understanding of 'accountability', typically in relation to public performance reporting. There were appeals for a guarantee that the results of the new standardised tests would not be used for school performance rankings. These points were also made in the stakeholder reflection seminar and are documented in Chapter 5.

> **Box 6.2. The central roles of schools and pedagogical advisory services in quality assurance**
>
> **Highly autonomous schools with responsibility to deliver quality education**
>
> Flemish schools are highly autonomous. This is underpinned by the constitution guaranteeing 'freedom of education'. 1 500 governing bodies or school boards (*inrichtende machten*) – responsible for one or more schools - receive public funding and can award official certificates or diplomas. They must follow a core curriculum set by the Flemish authorities and allow the inspection of their schools. Since 2009, schools have legal responsibility for providing good quality education. However, each school is free to determine the definition of 'quality'.
>
> In practice, reports from Flemish school principals in the PISA 2015 survey, show that school boards largely delegate responsibilities to the school principal and, regarding choosing textbooks and determining course content, teachers carry the main responsibilities (OECD, 2016[10]). School boards retain considerable responsibility with respect to budgetary matters and firing teachers (around half of the participating students were in schools where this was reported). Decisions related to teachers' salaries (which are not the responsibility of schools) is the only area where Flemish schools have less autonomy than on average in the OECD.
>
> **Different pedagogical advisory services offering support to schools**
>
> School boards may choose to affiliate with an umbrella organisation. With the exception of the Consultation Body of Small Education Providers (*Overleg Kleine Onderwijsverstrekkers*), each umbrella organisation provides its own pedagogical advisory service, PBD (*pedagogische begeleidingsdienst*). The PBD are long established and have been considered "among the most important partners of schools in quality assurance" (Ministry of Education and Training and the University of Antwerp, 2010[11]). In practice, school boards may surrender some of their autonomy to their umbrella organisation by using a curriculum, assessment or quality assurance tools it has developed. Notably, standardised tests are developed and offered by the PBD of both Catholic Education Flanders, KOV (*Katholiek Onderwijs Vlaanderen*) and the Educational Secretariat of the Association of Flemish Cities and Municipalities, OVSG (*Onderwijssecretariaat voor Steden en Gemeenten van de Vlaamse Gemeenschap*) (see Chapter 5).

At the same time, the OECD team noted a demand for regular reliable information on schools. Freedom of education applies both to the freedom for providers to establish schools based on particular values and goals, as well as parents choosing a school for their children according to their respective values. On this latter point, the OECD team noted arguments made by parental and student representatives that schools could better meet responsibilities on communicating about the quality of their educational provision. There is a lack of information on school quality to support school choice. They noted that the current health crisis had brought an additional challenge due to fewer physical visits and greater reliance on consulting online materials. There was an appreciation for the public availability of school inspection reports, but points were made about their limited usefulness, in terms of many being outdated (due to the inspection review cycle), only limited information is included in the public report and the reporting style is not easily navigated.

The 'quality triangle' approach is embedded, but there are some frustrations

The major mechanism to hold schools accountable is the Flemish Education Inspectorate (the Inspectorate). Established in 1991, it is an independent body under the direct jurisdiction of the Minister of Education. The inspectorate evaluates whether schools adhere to regulations and achieve minimum standards around quality and processes in place (attainment targets). The role of school inspection as a major element of accountability in Flemish education was not questioned in any of the discussions with the OECD team.

Together with schools and their pedagogical advisory services (PBD), the Inspectorate forms a pillar of the 'quality triangle' in Flemish education. The OECD team noted during discussions with stakeholders that the established 'quality triangle' approach was firmly rooted in the educational culture. All stakeholders were familiar with this, referred to it with ease and used it as the 'anchor' of many of their arguments. It was seen to fit well with the constitutional freedom of education, placing responsibility for education quality firmly with the schools. At the same time, the OECD team noted some frustrations relating to the implementation of the quality triangle and how professionals could intervene with their respective roles. Specifically, representatives from the Inspectorate and the umbrella organisations were hopeful that the availability of results from standardised tests could strengthen the reactivity and implementation of each part of the quality triangle.

The OECD team attempts to present visually the points raised about how the quality triangle currently works (Figure 6.2). On the left side of the triangle, the Inspectorate interacts with all schools (as a condition to receive public funding), as indicated by the blue arrow. However, the length and narrowness of the arrow represents the distance of this relationship due to the length of the inspection cycle, which leaves a lag in feedback for schools, parents and students on school quality. The Inspectorate could benefit from seeing how schools integrate standardised tests to their quality assurance processes and from the availability of regular information on school outcomes. This would strengthen the evidence base for inspectors and, as representatives from the Inspectorate commented in the stakeholder reflection seminar, support the implementation of a more differentiated inspection approach (see Chapter 5). In essence, this relates to greater reactivity from the inspectorate to intervene in a more timely way in schools with educational quality concerns.

On the right side of the triangle, there are looser connections, as autonomous schools may choose whether or not to engage support. The exception is a direct accountability mechanism by which the Inspectorate may obligate schools to engage external support, in the case that inspection processes have identified quality concerns. In reality, there are strong and more frequent connections between many schools and their pedagogical advisory services, indicated by the shorter and wider arrow. However, there are some significant 'support gaps'. Not all schools belong to an umbrella organisation that offers pedagogical advisory services. This is the case for the umbrella organisation for smaller, independent schools and it often reflects the diversity in nature of their particular pedagogical identities, e.g. Steiner schools. Representatives from all umbrella organisations noted the varying capacity of schools to work with quality assurance. This is borne out in evidence from school inspections (see Chapter 5).

The work of the pedagogical advisory services is demand driven; which means that they mainly work with those schools that are open to support. Some underlined frustrations with the limited reach for their pedagogical advisors in schools that may benefit from their support, but which do not look for it. Representatives from the Flemish Provincial Education (POV) advised that the network had invested significant time in nurturing relationships with its schools to close effectively this 'support gap' over recent years, building trust in the value of the support it offers. There was a recognition within some umbrella organisations of examining how they could sharpen their own approaches. Representatives from the KOV underlined the greater focus on accountability within the pedagogical advisory services for the effectiveness of the support they offered.

Figure 6.2. The triangle of educational quality in Flanders

OECD team analysis of the current connections among the three major pillars

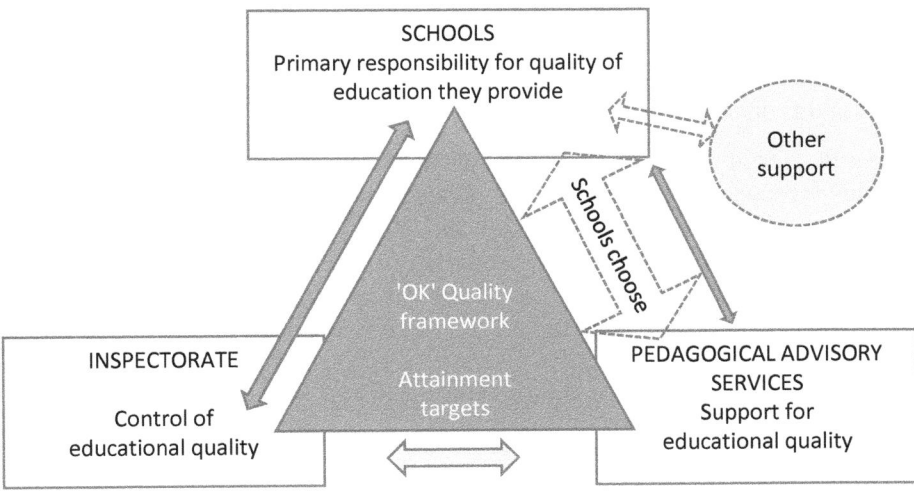

Note: At the top of the triangle are autonomous schools, legally responsible for the quality of their provision. Elements in blue are underpinned by regulation. Within the main triangle, schools are legally required to ensure that their students achieve the attainment targets. Schools are obliged to receive an inspection from the Inspectorate. The arrow is long and narrow indicating the long school inspection cycle. The Inspectorate can obligate a school to engage external support to improve the quality of its educational offer. However, in reality this is rarely implemented. All umbrella organisations, except for small school providers, offer educational support via Pedagogical advisory services (PBD). Schools can choose to use the curriculum developed by the PBD and also to use standardised tests, currently developed by two of the PBD. In reality, many schools choose support from the PBD. The arrow, therefore, indicates stronger and closer connections, although these remain trust based and voluntary. Representatives from the Inspectorate and the PBD report that there are strengthened professional connections between their respective roles since the coconstruction of the 'OK' Quality framework (*Referentiekader Onderwijskwaliteit*). OK is the Dutch acronym for educational quality.

Schools are responsible for the quality of the education they provide and standardised tests will provide regular information in a comparative light. This is expected to stimulate more critical self-reflection and professional discussion. However, Pedagogical Advisory Services see a role to support schools in contextualising and interpreting the results of standardised tests, and implementing concrete actions to improve quality. Representatives report that schools and teachers are extremely comfortable with summative assessment for students, but less familiar with using evidence for discussion on school development. Some networks reported they had invested in working with schools to analyse feedback, whether from their own standardised tests, the central assessments (*peilingen*) or international assessments, so this will provide fertile ground for working with the results of the new standardised tests. See also Chapter 5 for an overview of varying school capacity.

At the base of the triangle, the OECD team reflects feedback during discussions with the inspectorate and the pedagogical advisory services on their strengthened professional ties. This is anchored in the recent co-construction of the OK quality framework and expectations for greater alignment in feedback to schools (see below). The development of the OK quality framework marks a significant shift in efforts to make accountability processes more meaningful for schools. Three major principles of this new inspection approach (*Inspectie 2.0*) introduced in September 2018 are that schools, pedagogical advisory services and the inspectorate share the same reference framework for education quality; that the inspectorate builds upon the school's internal quality assurance; and that the inspectorate minimises administrative burden for schools (Flemish Education Inspectorate, 2018[12]). As this is progressively rolled out, the expectation is that the connections on all sides of the triangle will be strengthened.

Appreciation that accountability is anchored in a broad definition of school quality

Although at relatively early stages of implementation, the OECD team noted high levels of appreciation for the OK quality framework as an anchor for school accountability and development processes. In particular, several stakeholders referred to the breadth of areas covered to capture 'school quality'. The OK framework was introduced two years ago and presents 37 areas of educational quality. During discussions with the OECD team, all stakeholders made the point that feedback from standardised tests should not distort or narrow this broader understanding of quality.

The OK quality framework is formulated "openly and invitingly" and encourages schools to develop their own quality policy and improvement path (Flemish Education Inspectorate and Flemish Ministry of Education and Training, 2018[13]). This embodies an important principle to promote functional accountability exchanges, as it establishes an agreement on core objectives and organises discretionary room for schools and the inspectorate. The focus of external evaluations on schools' process of self-evaluation, rather than their content also enables schools to develop their education quality along local notions.

During discussions with the OECD team, parental representatives voiced support for this broad definition of school quality and how it provided common guidance for all Flemish schools and networks. Earlier OECD reviews on evaluation and assessment in OECD countries had pointed to the importance of promoting a 'common language' for all aspects of school evaluation (OECD, 2013[14]). Representatives from the different umbrella organisations reported that the development and ongoing implementation of the OK quality framework had 'eased tensions' between these two pillars of the quality triangle (Figure 6.2). However, teacher union representatives still perceive the quality framework as 'too removed' from the work of teachers, although they noted that this may become more familiar over coming years.

Organising agreement and areas of disagreements on expectations of education is a challenging process, yet an essential foundation for more constructive accountability relationships that promote learning. Accountability is an often-conflictual enterprise and across the public sector, there are often disputes over the substantive goals and how success should be measured (Overman, 2020[15]; Olsen, 2013[5]). All the more true in education, as it is a field with strong beliefs, tied to identities and experiences. These values and identities shape the objectives stakeholders expect education to deliver (Burns, Köster and Fuster, 2016[16]; Hooge, 2016[17]). In such a context, mobilising agreement among stakeholders on a fundamental set of objectives is instrumental to more constructive accountability relationships – even if they disagree on other objectives (Blanc, 2018[18]; Lind and Tyler, 1988[19]). At the core of the OK quality framework is the concept 'development of the learner', which generated a broad support base. The development of the framework represents a considerable achievement in the Flemish education system which is traditionally rooted in 'freedom of education'.

Previous work within the OECD strategic education governance project has highlighted the development of the OK quality framework as an exemplary initiative towards a more systemic and system-wide evaluation practice and an excellent opportunity to build trust and create ownership of schools and teachers (Shewbridge, Fuster and Rouw, 2019[2]). Despite efforts in the past to communicate and publish the former 'CIPO' inspection framework (quality indicators for school context, input, processes and output), schools were not very acquainted with it (Shewbridge et al., 2011[20]). A long inspection cycle (every 10 years) and a deliberate approach not to focus on school self-evaluation compounded the remoteness of the inspection framework from the daily work of schools. It may have led to costly duplication of data gathering and evaluation processes in schools and significantly reduced the potential of inspections to help schools build their evaluative capacity and report progress effectively.

The development of the OK quality framework was conceived as a partnership to develop a common vision and placed priority on stakeholder involvement. A first step in developing the framework consisted of an in depth literature review and an extensive stakeholder survey during the 2016-17 school year. This gathered feedback from pupils and students, parents, teachers and school leaders, pedagogical advisors, teacher trainers, education inspectors, experts and trade unions. The stakeholder feedback and research review played an important role in the development of the framework and are summarised in the background 'sources' report (*Bronnendocument referentiekader voor onderwijskwaliteit*) (Flemish Education Inspectorate and Flemish Ministry of Education and Training, 2018[13]).

This broad ownership of the OK quality framework is a solid basis to promote more constructive accountability relationships in the Flemish system. Having a broad agreement on substantive expectations can lessen the frustrations experienced when accountability is perceived to be purely based on compliancy. If a forum believes an actor does not work towards the forum's substantive expectations or does not share the same priorities, forums tend to focus on ensuring compliance and are more likely to concentrate on enforcing more defensible, less ambiguous, and more readily demonstrable standards (Busuioc and Lodge, 2016[21]; Overman, 2020[15]; Behn, 2001[22]). In a climate in which forums focus on enforcing compliance, actors may choose to carry out their substantive work in ways that is most defensible to minimise the chance of breaches. They may feel compelled to preserve the status quo rather than taking the risks necessary to learn what is optimal (Smith, 1995[23]).

Professional dialogue and rich feedback are valued in inspection processes

Several stakeholders described to the OECD team how the inspection approach had moved towards placing more emphasis on feedback for school development. Prior to 1991, there was one entity inspecting and advising Flemish schools, however the Constitutional Court declared that the Inspectorate had a strict evaluation purpose and could not go beyond a good or bad evaluation judgement. This led to a strict division, for several decades, between the inspectors controlling schools and umbrella organisations supporting schools. However, reportedly, this strictly evaluative form of inspection had not brought new information or insight for schools, it simply documented what they already knew. This gave rise to feedback that inspection did not have much impact on school practices or lead to educational change (Penninckx et al., 2015[24]). Regardless of the reason for it, an accountability exchange focusing on strict compliance can 'hollow out' the exchange. It can limit reflection on substantive conduct and lead to less information about practice from which to learn (Behn, 2001[22]).

The evolution of the Flemish Inspectorate's approach has sought to address concerns raised by stakeholders, namely their need to learn more from the inspection process. The Flemish Inspectorate has put stronger focus on the importance of professional dialogue – indeed its strapline is "Inspecting in dialogue (*Doorlichten in dialoog*)" – and trained inspectors in how to improve feedback to school principals and teachers. This is in line with the general consensus among the European professional network of school inspectors (SICI) that 'the more communication there is, the more trust there is between teachers, schools and inspectors' (Manes-Bonnisseau, 2019[25]). Engaging in meaningful professional dialogue can support a more functional accountability relationship. It can help align substantive expectations for the accountability exchange and create a mutual perception of working towards a common 'greater good' (Fry, 1995[26]; Fahey and Köster, 2019[3]).

While teacher unions made the point that they 'would always be critical of inspection', during discussions with the OECD team they also communicated respect for the rich feedback from inspectors rooted in professional dialogue. This would seem to indicate that the inspectorate strapline of "inspecting in dialogue" is communicated through actual inspection processes and appreciated by educators. Recent research found that teachers in Flemish primary schools were generally positive about feedback from school inspections, but in particular noted the importance of the perceived relevance of the feedback teachers received (Quintelier, De Maeyer and Vanhoof, 2020[27]).

The inclusion of former school leaders within the inspectorate can support the credibility of the inspection processes among educational professionals. This can support more functional and meaningful accountability exchanges (Figure 6.1). If actors consider a given forum as authoritative and legitimate to inquire about a specific work, they tend to render accounts more completely and accurately in the accountability exchange. In the context of performance feedback, this had been found to promote critical reflection on substantive work (Mero, Guidice and Brownlee, 2007[28]; Curtis, Harvey and Ravden, 2005[29]). Conversely, when actors do not consider those holding them to account as capable, any input from accountability exchanges is more easily dismissed (Fahey and Köster, 2019[3]).

References

Behn, R. (2001), *Rethinking democratic accountability*, Brookings Institution Press, https://www.jstor.org/stable/10.7864/j.ctvdf03r8. [22]

Blanc, F. (2018), "Tools for Effective Regulation: Is "More" Always "Better"?", *European Journal of Risk Regulation*, Vol. 9/3, pp. 465-482, http://dx.doi.org/10.1017/err.2018.19. [18]

Burns, T., F. Köster and M. Fuster (2016), *Education Governance in Action: Lessons from Case Studies*, Educational Research and Innovation, OECD Publishing, Paris, https://dx.doi.org/10.1787/9789264262829-en. [16]

Busuioc, M. and M. Lodge (2016), "Reputation and Accountability Relationships: Managing Accountability Expectations through Reputation", *Public Administration Review*, Vol. 77/1, pp. 91-100, http://dx.doi.org/10.1111/puar.12612. [21]

Curtis, A., R. Harvey and D. Ravden (2005), "Sources of Political Distortions in Performance Appraisals", *Group & Organization Management*, Vol. 30/1, pp. 42-60, http://dx.doi.org/10.1177/1059601104267666. [29]

Fahey, G. and F. Köster (2019), "Means, ends and meaning in accountability for strategic education governance", *OECD Education Working Papers*, No. 204, OECD Publishing, Paris, https://dx.doi.org/10.1787/1d516b5c-en. [3]

Flemish Education Inspectorate (2018), *Inspection profiles - Flanders*. [12]

Flemish Education Inspectorate and Flemish Ministry of Education and Training (2018), *Sources document: reference framework for education quality (Bronnendocument: Referentiekader voor ondewijskwaliteit)*, https://www.onderwijsinspectie.be/sites/default/files/atoms/files/OK_bronnendoc_LOW_14-10-2019.pdf. [13]

Fry, R. (1995), "Accountability in organizational life: Problem or opportunity for nonprofits?", *Nonprofit Management and Leadership*, Vol. 6/2, pp. 181-195, http://dx.doi.org/10.1002/nml.4130060207. [26]

Gelfand, M., B. Lim and J. Raver (2004), "Culture and accountability in organizations: Variations in forms of social control across cultures", *Human Resource Management Review*, Vol. 14/1, pp. 135-160, http://dx.doi.org/10.1016/j.hrmr.2004.02.007. [9]

Hooge, E. (2016), "Making multiple school accountability work", in *Governing Education in a Complex World*, OECD Publishing, Paris, https://dx.doi.org/10.1787/9789264255364-7-en. [17]

Lanivich, S. et al. (2010), "P-E Fit as moderator of the accountability – employee reactions relationships: Convergent results across two samples", *Journal of Vocational Behavior*, Vol. 77/3, pp. 425-436, http://dx.doi.org/10.1016/j.jvb.2010.05.004. [8]

Lind, E. and T. Tyler (1988), "Introduction", in *The Social Psychology of Procedural Justice, Critical Issues in Social Justice*, Springer US, Boston, MA, http://dx.doi.org/10.1007/978-1-4899-2115-4_1. [19]

Manes-Bonnisseau, C. (2019), *SICI president, Standing International Conference of Inspectorates (SICI)*, https://www.sici-inspectorates.eu/Activities/Development-and-Research/Thematic-reports/Innovative-practices-of-inspection (accessed on February 2020). [25]

Mero, N., R. Guidice and A. Brownlee (2007), "Accountability in a Performance Appraisal Context: The Effect of Audience and Form of Accounting on Rater Response and Behavior", *Journal of Management*, Vol. 33/2, pp. 223-252, http://dx.doi.org/10.1177/0149206306297633. [28]

Ministry of Education and Training and the University of Antwerp (2010), *Country Background Report for the Flemish Community of Belgium: OECD Reviews on Evaluation and Assessment Frameworks for Improving School Outcomes*, http://www.oecd.org/education/school/46974684.pdf. [11]

OECD (2016), *PISA 2015 Results (Volume II): Policies and Practices for Successful Schools*, PISA, OECD Publishing, Paris, https://dx.doi.org/10.1787/9789264267510-en. [10]

OECD (2013), *Synergies for Better Learning: An International Perspective on Evaluation and Assessment*, OECD Reviews of Evaluation and Assessment in Education, OECD Publishing, Paris, https://dx.doi.org/10.1787/9789264190658-en. [14]

Olsen, J. (2013), "The Institutional Basis of Democratic Accountability", *West European Politics*, Vol. 36/3, pp. 447-473, http://dx.doi.org/10.1080/01402382.2012.753704. [5]

Overman, S. (2020), "Aligning accountability arrangements for ambiguous goals: the case of museums", *Public Management Review*, pp. 1-21, http://dx.doi.org/10.1080/14719037.2020.1722210. [15]

Penninckx, M. et al. (2015), "Explaining effects and side effects of school inspections: a path analysis", *School Effectiveness and School Improvement*, Vol. 27/3, pp. 333-347, http://dx.doi.org/10.1080/09243453.2015.1085421. [24]

Quintelier, A., S. De Maeyer and J. Vanhoof (2020), "The role of feedback acceptance and gaining awareness on teachers' willingness to use inspection feedback", *Educational Assessment, Evaluation and Accountability*, Vol. 32/3, pp. 311-333, http://dx.doi.org/10.1007/s11092-020-09325-9. [27]

Rouw, R. et al. (2016), "United in Diversity: A Complexity Perspective on the Role of Attainment Targets in Quality Assurance in Flanders", *OECD Education Working Papers*, No. 139, OECD Publishing, Paris, https://dx.doi.org/10.1787/5jlrb8ftvqs1-en. [1]

Schillemans, T. and M. Busuioc (2014), "Predicting Public Sector Accountability: From Agency Drift to Forum Drift", *Journal of Public Administration Research and Theory*, Vol. 25/1, pp. 191-215, http://dx.doi.org/10.1093/jopart/muu024. [6]

Schillemans, T. and R. Smulders (2015), "Learning From Accountability?! Whether, What, and When", *Public Performance & Management Review*, Vol. 39/1, pp. 248-271, http://dx.doi.org/10.1080/15309576.2016.1071175. [4]

Shewbridge, C., M. Fuster and R. Rouw (2019), "Constructive accountability, transparency and trust between government and highly autonomous schools in Flanders", *OECD Education Working Papers*, No. 199, OECD Publishing, Paris, https://dx.doi.org/10.1787/c891abbf-en. [2]

Shewbridge, C. et al. (2011), *OECD Reviews of Evaluation and Assessment in Education: School Evaluation in the Flemish Community of Belgium 2011*, OECD Reviews of Evaluation and Assessment in Education, OECD Publishing, Paris, https://dx.doi.org/10.1787/9789264116726-en. [20]

Smith, P. (1995), "On the unintended consequences of publishing performance data in the public sector", *International Journal of Public Administration*, Vol. 18/2-3, pp. 277-310, http://dx.doi.org/10.1080/01900699508525011. [23]

Stacey, R. (1995), "The Science of Complexity: An Alternative Perspective for Strategic Change Processes", Vol. 16/6, pp. 477-495, https://doi.org/10.1002/smj.4250160606. [7]

7 Lessons from the OECD case study

This Chapter presents a brief overview of lessons learnt in the OECD case study. For each domain of the strategic education governance framework, it presents some key points and reflections on what these imply for the further development of standardised tests.

Stakeholder involvement (Chapter 3)

Prioritising clear and active communication

The OECD case study has identified unclear communication as a point of weakness in the initial stages of developing standardised tests. The establishment of the high-level forum is a constructive step. This can serve as an authoritative communication channel at key stages in the development of the standardised tests and also collect feedback in a timely and transparent way from key stakeholders. It can also be a platform for expert contributions and testimonies from the educational field as the project unfolds.

The overriding feedback from stakeholders in the OECD case study, including from test developers, is the need for a clear steer from the central authorities on the purpose(s) of the standardised tests. There is opportunity to more actively involve stakeholders in the next stage of development, such as to provide input into clarifying the purpose(s) and uses of the standardised tests. This will pave the way to enable stakeholders to take up their roles and responsibilities in preparing for the introduction of standardised tests.

Committing to stakeholder involvement and ensuring key voices are heard

Educational policy development in Flanders has a tradition of involving different stakeholders (especially umbrella organisations in school networks and trade unions). Stakeholders were strongly critical about a lack of consultation processes at the early stages of the introduction of the standardised tests. An important lesson for the government is to take stakeholder involvement seriously at every stage of the policy development.

One important group of stakeholders tends to be overlooked: the school leaders. The absence of a representative body for school leaders weakens this important voice in official channels to support policy development. There is a need to reflect on ways to systematically involve school leaders, for example, with a rotating representation of school leaders from each network in the high-level forum. There are ways to mobilise existing professional connections with the pedagogical advisory services and going forward, as suggested below, via direct interactions with the university centre. Mobilising awareness, support and feedback channels for school leaders will be critical to the successful introduction of the standardised tests.

Ensuring facilitative leadership

The OECD case study has identified much motivation among stakeholders for greater and more structured involvement in the introduction of standardised tests. Strong technical credibility in facilitative leadership can help heighten the engagement of different stakeholder groups. Here, the strong credibility for the university centre as a centre of scientific expertise will provide fertile ground for gaining regular feedback from the educational field during test development.

The department can take the opportunity to empower student voice by supporting the Flemish Student Association's suggestion to conduct a survey among its membership. This can be a way to seek feedback on key aspects of the standardised tests development.

Organising contributions from the educational field to support the university centre

There is motivation for involvement in test development and opportunity in establishing a coalition of test development partners across educational networks to support the university centre's work. The university centre can facilitate this by providing clear guidance on scheduling and expected time commitments. The pedagogical advisory services can facilitate and organise the participation of expert teachers and schools. It will be important to engage expertise from teachers and the test developers in the pedagogical advisory services to support the development of specific test items in Dutch and mathematics. There is also a need to engage school leaders and other staff in designing and developing the feedback reports for schools. The development of standardised tests presents an opportunity to bring schools together across different networks and strengthen horizontal collaboration. This interaction between test developers and test users (schools) is an important research-based principle of supporting more systematic use of evidence.

Strategic thinking and whole-of-system perspective (Chapter 4)

Developing, sharing and consolidating common goals and how standardised tests will support these

The OECD case study has found that there is a shared concern on the overall quality of education in Flanders and a body of evidence to support this. Such widespread recognition is pivotal and presents an opportunity to mobilise stakeholders in creating a common vision for the role of standardised tests in supporting the quality of educational provision going forward. The OECD case study has found enthusiasm for the opportunities that standardised tests could offer. There is strong support for a vision of standardised tests as tools to support school quality development. In contrast, stakeholders were unanimous in voicing concern on the eventual publication of results of these tests as indicators of school performance. It is important to consider safeguard measures to support the use of data for school development, including to ensure schools are encouraged to continue to develop and innovate their practice.

Taking a long-term perspective and adapting to changing contexts and new knowledge

The development and introduction of standardised tests in Flanders is a groundbreaking project. The OECD case study has revealed a gradual evolution in attitudes towards the potential that standardised tests could bring for Flemish schools and enthusiasm among many stakeholders. There is value in taking a long-term perspective on the introduction of standardised tests and refining and evolving their development through concrete experiences in the educational field. First, the development of the standardised tests presents an opportunity to bring together the research community (test developers) and schools. Such collaboration will provide many other advantages for professional learning and development on both sides. Once developed, the initial introduction of standardised tests will bring new experiences and opportunities for rich, concrete feedback from the broader educational field. The first few administrations of the standardised tests will generate much knowledge for how to optimise the use of results at the school level.

There would be value in considering (and consulting about) how the introduction of standardised tests will be placed within the context of school (self) improvement processes and practices – as well as broader education strategic planning initiatives to support schools in their ongoing development. For example, standardised tests can be used to develop curriculum as well as monitor equity gaps over time for specific groups, which can then lead to higher-level strategic supports to be implemented. A clear opportunity to solidify initial expectations is to ensure a coherent approach and communication from the Flemish education inspectorate and the pedagogical advisory services on how to use these results for school development as part of the broader view of educational quality (anchored in the 'OK' quality framework).

Coordinating action and learning from experiences in the educational field

The OECD case study has noted that there is a complex and healthy debate on the reasons for the observed decline in the overall quality of education in Flanders. Feedback from the educational field highlights growing concerns on the prestige of the teaching profession and quite some variation in openness to change among Flemish schools, particularly between the primary and secondary levels. These points indicate a need to carefully establish positive experiences with the standardised tests in the educational field and to nurture support for these as effective and relevant educational tools for professionals.

The working realities for teachers necessitate a coordinated guidance from the central authorities on the expected use of the standardised tests and the associated time and resource requirements for teachers and schools. This needs to be based on systematic input from the educational field on their requirements and experiences as the standardised tests are being developed and introduced.

Capacity and knowledge governance (Chapter 5)

Ensuring technical capacity for standardised test development and administration

The OECD case study has identified much motivation among stakeholders for greater and more structured involvement in the introduction of standardised tests. Strong technical credibility in facilitative leadership can help heighten the engagement of different stakeholder groups. Here, the strong credibility for the university centre as a centre of scientific expertise will provide fertile ground for gaining regular feedback from the educational field during test development.

The OECD case study has noted some concerns and supporting evidence on the capacity to administer digital tests across Flemish schools. There will need to be a careful evaluation of schools' capacity to administer digital tests and due attention to field trials when first administering the tests.

Laying foundations for the systematic use of standardised test results by professionals

The OECD case study has documented the major motivations for the introduction of standardised tests. Feedback from stakeholders suggests that standardised tests would be most valuable as tools to: provide reliable information on outcomes for students, teachers and schools; provide comparative feedback to schools for reflection on their development; strengthen and promote a culture of feedback for student learning; deepen professionals' skills for using data and evidence more systematically; provide data for educational research and policy; and augment the evidence base for school inspections. There is opportunity to use the motivations identified by the stakeholder groups to develop clear, comprehensible feedback reports for schools. In preparing for the use of test results, feedback from stakeholders notes the necessity for: a clear and uniform communication strategy; planning time and resources in schools; preparing guidance for schools; and supporting professionals. The OECD case study allows a mapping of these points to the research-based framework supporting a more systematic use of evidence by decision makers in their work.

Skills: There is a need to give adequate attention to the capabilities of teachers and other school staff to work with the results of standardised tests and other assessments. For teachers, to use these as one form of evidence to give feedback to students and parents on learning progress. At the school level, to interpret the results for the school in light of central benchmarks and to feed this into plans for school development. Teachers voiced the opportunities for deepening professional skills in using data. There is opportunity in committing to investment in professional development and in ways that can support collaborative practices in schools.

Availability: The standardised tests present an opportunity to make available regular and reliable student performance data to schools in the common areas of mathematics and Dutch. The OECD case study documents that the rapidity of results feedback will play into their perceived value and relevance for educators. Notably, students expressed a desire for the standardised tests to bolster the culture of feedback to students on their progress more generally and more rapid feedback would best support this.

Organisational processes: School leaders will drive the preparation of the necessary processes and structures to create the space for effective use of the standardised tests. This can be supported at the system level by preparation of common guidance material for schools – a process that will need to engage school leaders and teachers in a structured way. As in all educational systems, capacities for quality assurance and development at the school level vary across Flemish schools. The OECD case study notes that evidence on school capacity from the Flemish education inspectorate is widely known and referred to by the majority of stakeholders. This indicates a maturity in the educational field as to recognising differing realities and starting points across schools. Notably, the pedagogical advisory services affiliated to the umbrella organisations have nurtured ties with many schools and in recent years have increased their focus on providing support to schools to improve their quality assurance processes. This knowledge and expertise can be tapped into when introducing the standardised tests.

Interaction: The design and development of feedback from the standardised tests will be strengthened by the direct interaction between researchers (analysts and feedback designers) and schools. Importantly, this presents an opportunity to promote horizontal collaboration and learning across the different educational networks.

Standards: The development of guidance material for schools will provide a common anchor for expectations on the use of standardised tests. This should clarify the ways that standardised tests are connected with the existing central anchors of the attainment targets and the broader 'OK' quality framework. There are roles here for the Flemish education inspectorate and the pedagogical advisory services to document expectations of how to best interpret the evidence provided by the standardised tests and how to position these in a broader array of evidence at the school level.

Accountability (Chapter 6)

Ensuring the 'fit' of accountability instruments

The OECD case study has noted the perception of 'accountability' in Flemish education as a matter of internal responsibility and great resistance to the public availability of school performance information. The development of the 'OK' quality framework represents a considerable achievement in the Flemish education system. By design, this framework embodies the organised agreement on expectations of school quality and also leaves the necessary room for disagreement and local flexibility in continuing to develop targeted quality goals for the school's specific community. The 'quality triangle' concept is embedded in the educational field, with the schools having the main responsibility for their educational quality, their pedagogical advisory services providing support and the Flemish education inspectorate as the major accountability mechanism. Professional dialogue and rich feedback are valued in inspection processes.

There is opportunity to place standardised tests within the strengths of the current accountability system that focuses on dialogue and deepening an understanding between available data and links to ideas for improving practice. The standardised tests offer opportunities to help 'firm up' two important sides of the quality triangle: inspection and pedagogical advisory services. On one side, the Flemish education inspectorate will benefit from the availability of regular, comparable information on student performance in two key areas. This will further enrich the evidence base for school inspections and may support greater reactivity by supporting the implementation of a differentiated approach to inspections. On the other side, the pedagogical advisory services will have a greater evidence base to work with schools seeking their support. In recent years, these services have increased their focus on supporting schools with their quality assurance processes. This would not change the existing accountability mechanism that allows the inspectorate to obligate a school with noted quality issues to engage with pedagogical support services and initiate an improvement trajectory. Both sides of the triangle will continue to anchor their work in the common 'OK' quality framework. This will be key to helping interpret and use the results of standardised tests in a constructive and proportionate way.

Enhancing critical reflection on substantive expectations

The development of standardised tests that provide common feedback to all Flemish schools will provide an objective and external perspective for school development. Schools carry the main responsibility for the quality of their educational provision. The availability of regular, reliable data on student performance with comparative benchmarks will be a basis to further strengthen their critical reflection. To fully support the learning function, there would be value in exploring mechanisms for designing data use and interpretation by teachers and school leaders to support informed practice and strategic planning.

In turn, the Flemish education inspectorate can confer a valuable perspective to schools on how to interpret and use the results of the standardised tests as part of their quality assurance processes. Regular exchanges with schools via school inspection processes will strengthen the knowledge and capacity of school inspectors regarding effective and innovative ways of working with the standardised tests at tools for school development.

www.ingramcontent.com/pod-product-compliance
Ingram Content Group UK Ltd.
Pitfield, Milton Keynes, MK11 3LW, UK
UKHW051300180426
11947UKWH00020B/1815